Spiritual Wisdom for Every Need and Occasion . . .

Lord, I have been fed with Your bounty,
Clothed with Your mercy,
Comforted by Your love,
Healed by Your grace,
And upheld by Your hand.

—Jarena Lee, the first female minister
in the African Methodist Episcopal Church

This beautiful collection of more than 300 prayers
can be used by the whole family to celebrate and affirm
a living faith—in times of reflection, thankfulness,
sorrow, and jubilation.

The REVEREND CHESTINA MITCHELL ARCHIBALD is a nationally
renowned minister and educator who is chaplain-in-residence at
Fisk University. A former member of the editorial board for
Gospel Today magazine and a writer for the National Baptist Pub-
lishing Board, she lives in Nashville.

Say
Amen!

THE
AFRICAN AMERICAN
FAMILY'S BOOK
OF PRAYERS

EDITED BY
REVEREND
CHESTINA MITCHELL ARCHIBALD

A PLUME BOOK

PLUME
Published by the Penguin Group
Penguin Putnam Inc., 375 Hudson Street,
New York, New York 10014, U.S.A.
Penguin Books Ltd, 27 Wrights Lane,
London W8 5TZ, England
Penguin Books Australia Ltd, Ringwood,
Victoria, Australia
Penguin Books Canada Ltd, 10 Alcorn Avenue,
Toronto, Ontario, Canada M4V 3B2
Penguin Books (N.Z.) Ltd, 182-190 Wairau Road,
Auckland 10, New Zealand

Penguin Books Ltd, Registered Offices:
Harmondsworth, Middlesex, England

Published by Plume, an imprint of Dutton NAL,
a member of Penguin Putnam Inc.
Previously published in a Dutton edition.

First Plume Printing, October, 1998
10 9 8 7 6

Ⓟ REGISTERED TRADEMARK—MARCA REGISTRADA

The Library of Congress has catalogued the Dutton edition as follows:

Say amen! : the African American family's book of prayers / edited by
   Chestina Mitchell Archibald.
      p. cm.
   ISBN 0-525-94215-7 (hc.)
   ISBN 0-452-27729-9 (pbk.)
   1. Afro-Americans—Prayer-books and devotions—English.   2. Afro-
American families—Religious life.   I. Archibald, Chestina
Mitchell.
BR563.N4S39   1997
242'.8—dc21   97-20403
                                                              CIP

Printed in the United States of America
Original hardcover produced by the Philip Lief Group, Inc.

BOOKS ARE AVAILABLE AT QUANTITY DISCOUNTS WHEN USED TO PROMOTE PRODUCTS OR SERVICES. FOR
INFORMATION PLEASE WRITE TO PREMIUM MARKETING DIVISION, PENGUIN PUTNAM INC.,
375 HUDSON STREET, NEW YORK, NEW YORK 10014.

This book is dedicated in loving memory of my parents, Mr. and Mrs. Thomas Mitchell, and my grandparents Mr. and Mrs. Edmond Horne, who insisted that prayer and church be a regular activity for the family; to my son, Albert John Archibald III, whose loving spirit is the manifestation of prayer; to my cousin, Reverend Chestina Delaney, who is my constant source of encouragement; and last but not least, to the students at Fisk University who are sources of inspiration and who have taught me much about prayer.

ACKNOWLEDGMENTS

Readers must realize that this book is the effort of many persons. I am deeply grateful to The Philip Lief Group for the book's concept and for providing invaluable assistance in mailing, editing, structuring, and research. Thanks to Deirdre Mullane of Dutton, who continued to require more. Thanks to John Young and Priscilla Agari, who gave stimulus for thought for many of the prayers on which my name appears, and to John and Judy Finn, who helped to compile the initial list of categories for prayers. Last but not least, thanks to the many contributors who took time to respond to the request for prayers.

CONTENTS

Prayers of Faith

FOR REFLECTION

FOR FORGIVENESS

Contents

Contents

ON SEEKING THE LORD'S PATH

Prayers for the Community

Prayers for Different Members of the Community

Prayers for the Family

Contents

Prayers for Special Events and Occasions

Prayers for Holidays and Other Special Days

Lord, I have been fed with Your bounty,
Clothed with Your mercy
Comforted by Your love
Healed by Your grace,
And upheld by Your hand.

—JARENA LEE,
the first female minister in the African Methodist Episcopal Church

INTRODUCTION

What Is Prayer?

Since the beginning of time, people have hungered for communication with their Creator, an effort collectively known as prayer. It is the soul's desire, expressed or unexpressed, to connect with the ultimate power of the universe. When prayer emanates from the soul, the heart is illuminated with divine inspiration. Throughout time, prayer has been called the key to the kingdom of God, and, as a key, prayer must be accompanied by the belief in a God who hears all adjurations and answers them according to His divine will. In addition, the presence of the Holy Spirit is needed. Prayer requires the engagement of both the soul and the Spirit; if one is absent, prayer becomes ineffective. It is the engagement of one's mind and soul that enables one to relinquish self-will and surrender to the will of the Creator. When one surrenders, the veil between the infinite and the finite is lifted; the division between the tangible and the intangible removed; and the distinction between the visible and the invisible erased. One experiences a transcendence of self and finds peace and comfort in the knowledge that the power of prayer and God's presence is touching every aspect of one's life.

When petitioning the ear of the Lord, one can choose from

many types of prayer for different needs and occasions in one's life: Intercessory prayers are used to pray for others; invocations are used to seek the presence of God; benedictions are offered when one wishes to ask for God's blessings; prayers of lamentation enable one to pour forth one's sorrow into the bosom of the Lord; and prayers of praise and thanksgiving acknowledge the wondrous works of an almighty God. Collectively, these bodies of prayer make up the prayer experience of the African American people. During our history, prayer has been one of our strongest weapons and at times our only weapon.

Prayer in the African American Community

Prayer has played a unique role in the lives of African Americans throughout history. It has brought forth results rivaled perhaps only by the release of the Israelites from Egyptian bondage. In both instances, enslaved people used prayer as their sole resource in securing freedom from human bondage. The first African Americans were without money, ammunition, and political clout; they were in a foreign country where they could barely speak the language and were forbidden by law to learn it. However, they were familiar with a tool that no law, principality, or human being could suppress. It was the power of prayer.

The first Africans brought to America knew of a God who eclipsed spatial and temporal boundaries. They called upon their God until they felt His presence and heard His voice echoed in their own as they sang praises to Him. With the sword of prayer, they escaped the institution of slavery and went on to achievements unthinkable in their former condition of servitude.

African Americans in this generation have also witnessed the power of prayer. Just as prayer caused slavery to be abolished, it also caused the walls of segregation to tumble like the walls of Jericho so that equal opportunities could be offered to all. God's ebony children knew the impact and the power of prayer. It has opened doors no human being could open. It has rolled back clouds, brought out sunshine, and caused disastrous storms to pass over. In retrospect, one sees that it was not the intensity of emotions but the depth of conviction that their cause was right and that God was on their side that gave African Americans the strength, courage, and fortitude to overcome insurmountable odds.

Who Is This Book For?

This distinctive compendium of prayers is designed for African Americans of all ages and Christian denominations. It will be helpful to both those who have accepted Jesus Christ as their personal savior and rest in that assurance and those who find their faith is faltering. It is suitable for both individuals and groups. Many will want to read these prayers aloud; others will want to use these prayers to silently address their everyday problems. People called upon to pray in public will also find it a unique source of inspiration.

In addition to helping in the formation of prayer, the material in this book should give readers hope in what sometimes appears to be a stark and faithless world. The need for prayer in our everyday lives is apparent. Whenever there is a crisis in the world, the masses rediscover the power of prayer. At present, African Americans are being challenged to return to the source of their strength and power. Having experienced a certain degree of human freedom, we seem to have almost turned our backs on the God of our deliverance. Like others, we have begun to serve idol gods such as materialism. This book is designed to help those who have repented and those who desire to repent in order to be restored to fellowship with God.

This book will also be useful to anyone searching for insight into the African American religious experience. Because African American religion has distinct expressions, to exclude it from any study of religion in America would be to dramatically distort a portrayal of American religion. Many of the historical prayers, infused with a cadence reminiscent of a heavenly band, are not only inspirational, but whisper of a time long gone. For example, a typical historical prayer might be a petition to God to help the person praying learn how to love not only his neighbor but also his neighbor's children as his own. Similarly, a person seeking moral instruction or desiring consolation or help in a time of need will find solace in the Prayers of Faith.

How This Book Is Structured

This book is organized into six categories: Prayers of Faith, Prayers for the Community, Prayers for Different Members of the Community, Prayers for the Family, Prayers for Special Events and Occasions, and Prayers for Holidays and Other Special Days. Included in Prayers of Faith are invocations aimed at helping one feel God's presence and strengthening one in moments of weakness. Situations unique to the African American community, ranging from church desecration to the celebration of African American pride, are addressed in Prayers for the Community. Prayers for professionals, such as teachers and ministers, and for travelers, retirees, prisoners, those living with HIV/AIDS, and many more are found in Prayers for Different Members of the Community. Tailored to specific family relationships, Prayers for the Family includes prayers about newborns as well as prayers for grandparents to say. Prayers for Special Events and Occasions range from a benediction for an opening assembly of government to grace at mealtime. Prayers for Holidays and Other Special Days contains prayers for both general holidays, such as Lent and New Year's Day, and African American holidays, such as Juneteenth and Kwanzaa.

Prayers in each category also have titles that will help users easily find what they need. For example, prayers falling within the Holidays and Other Special Days section are ordered chronologically according to both the secular and church calendars.

The prayers in this collection were selected to help readers build a stronger and more rewarding relationship with God and share in the rich prayer tradition of the African American people. It is my sincere wish that many will find this book helpful in creating an intimate and sacred reality of perpetual devotion.

—REVEREND CHESTINA MITCHELL ARCHIBALD
Fisk University, Nashville, Tennessee

Prayers of Faith

Without faith, it is impossible to please God.
HEBREWS 11:6

And this is the confidence that we have in Him, that, if we ask any thing according to His will, He heareth us.
1 JOHN 5:14

FOR REFLECTION

A PRAYER FOR PRAYER

Lord God, grant us to see that even as the Word must become flesh, the prayer must become physical: grant our prayers eyes to see the invisible, ears to hear the inaudible, minds to fathom the unknowable, hearts to feel the untouchable, lips to voice the unspeakable, hands to clutch the intangible. Then to complete the body of yearning, equip our prayers with legs to step out on faith, legs to progress one step at a time, legs to walk with our Savior in answering our very own askings. In the name of Jesus Christ.

Amen.

—REVEREND CECIL L. MURRAY

When Reverend Murray first came to the oldest black congregation in Los Angeles, the First African Methodist Episcopal Church, in 1977, he had a congregation of three hundred; today, the congregation consists of more than 12,300 members and has over thirty task forces that deal with a range of issues, from job testing and placement programs to a $5 million transportation program for seniors and the handicapped, to providing housing for the homeless. Reverend Murray has been an adjunct professor and has lectured at several universities and seminaries. He also served ten years on active duty in the U.S. Air Force.

ASKINGS

Omniscient One,
You know our often requests—
our self-serving wants—
that are hard for us to weed out
from our needs,
and how so often in our pleadings
we forget about your will
as we petition for
me, myself and mine.

But, you, we worship,
are above this limitedness—divine,
so as we pray
we are seeking your direction,
to think also of others,
who are not to us selfishly connected,
and to make our pleas
what you want.

Help us to seek
above all else
your kingdom.

—REVEREND WILL E. CHAMBERS

"Askings" is the first section of a larger work, *Prayer Portions*, which, Mr. Chambers says, "helps me focus my attitude in areas that are regularly part of my prayer life." He is currently presiding elder at the Christian Methodist Episcopal Church in Winston-Salem, North Carolina, and he supervises thirty-two Christian Methodist congregations in the Carolinas.

UNSPOKEN PRAYERS

I asked my God for strength,
that I might achieve . . .

I was made weak,
that I might humbly learn to obey.

I asked for health,
that I might do greater things . . .

I was given infirmity,
that I might do better things.

I asked for riches,
that I might be happy . . .

I was given poverty,
that I might be wise.

I asked for power,
that I might have the praise of men . . .

I was given weakness,
that I might feel the need of God.

I asked for all things,
that I might enjoy life . . .

I was given life,
that I might enjoy all things.

I got nothing that I asked for,
but everything I had hoped for.

Almost despite myself,
my unspoken prayers were answered.

I am among all men, most richly blessed!

—ANONYMOUS

This prayer illustrates how God does not always give us what we ask for. Instead, He gives us what He knows we need, whether we realize it at the time or not.

THE MYSTERY OF GOD

Dear God,
Let me not be afraid of that which I do not know, for even though I do not know what tomorrow holds, I know who holds tomorrow. I know You exist, Lord. I have seen Your mighty works and have felt Your presence. Yet, You remain a mystery, and it becomes increasingly difficult to explain You in a global society that is multicultural. There are things about You that we will not know or understand while on this earth. Lord, I do not fret over the unknown aspects of Your character; rather, I rejoice at each revelation of Your deep love and ardent involvement with our lives, for each glimpse of Your glory confirms that You are—that remains enough for me. In the beginning You were, in the end You shall be. In Christ's Name.
    Amen.

—REVEREND CHESTINA MITCHELL ARCHIBALD

In writing this prayer, Reverend Archibald found inspiration from Isaiah 55:8: "For my thoughts are not your thoughts, neither are your ways my ways, saith the Lord." The prayer illustrates how a strong faith in God need not be based on what we can see with our eyes—His powerful love and continuous guidance are confirmation enough.

LORD, LET ME HEAR YOU IN THE SILENCE

Sometimes I feel that words are not enough to express the soul. Sometimes silence has more power than speech. Guide me to talk only when necessary and at other times simply meditate or reflect to allow Your love to flow into my spirit. Endless chatter fills the time but not the void in my heart. Please quiet my mind that I may hear Your voice and be filled with Your precious essence which mere words cannot embrace. In Christ's Name.

    Amen.

—REVEREND CHESTINA MITCHELL ARCHIBALD

Reverend Archibald was inspired by Psalms 46:10a when writing this prayer: "Be still, and know that I am God." Outside noise can drown out God's voice, so we must take time for silence in order to hear God's word.

TRINITY

Lord God,

I pray for a clear understanding of the meaning of the Trinity. Many explain it in different ways, yet none make it plain. I know in my heart the true reality of a triune God. Help me to convey to all Your nature, the nature of Jesus, and the nature of the Holy Spirit. Help us to more deeply connect to You and to decipher the truths offered us through Your word, that we might be strengthened and become recipients of Your blessings. "Guide us O Thou great Jehovah" as we make our pilgrimage through this barren land. We are weak, but Thou art mighty—hold us with Thy powerful hand.

    Amen.

—REVEREND CHESTINA MITCHELL ARCHIBALD

This prayer was based on Luke 1:35: "And the angel answered and said unto her, the Holy Ghost shall come upon thee, and the power of the Highest shall overshadow thee: therefore also that holy thing which shall be born of thee shall be called the Son of God." While it is difficult for people to understand the mystery of the trinity, we know that all will eventually be revealed.

FATHER GOD, I COME TO YOU TODAY

Father God, I come to you today,
For grace and peace and joy I pray.
That which You have in store for me,
Comes to me instantly and constantly.
The things I need I do decree,
Not beg and cry for on my knee.
Since the Bible says that ye are God's,
I know that I can beat the odds.
     Amen.

—REVEREND RUN

Born Joseph Simmons, Reverend Run is best known as Run of the legendary and highly influential hip-hop group Run DMC. After he began attending services in 1990 at Zoe Ministries, a nondenominational church in New York City, he went on to become a deacon and was finally ordained as a minister in 1995. In addition to his continuing involvement with Run DMC, Reverend Run has started his own gospel record label, Rev Run Records, preaches occasionally at Zoe Ministries, and has been involved in various side projects. Reverend Run and his family reside in New York City.

I Need to Feel Your Presence, Lord

O Benevolent God,
I thank You for lifting my woeful spirit and filling the void in my heart with Your holy presence. When I feel alone and empty, Lord, let me always feel Your all-powerful presence within me and surrounding me, filling me with life anew. In Christ's Name.

Amen.

—Reverend Chestina Mitchell Archibald

Even in the face of doubt, we must trust that God is with us. In this way we begin to understand the meaning of faith, the pathway through which the Divine reveals itself. "They that wait upon the Lord shall renew their strength" (Isaiah 40:31).

PRAYER FOR DISCOVERY

Father, I thank you that before we ever begin our search for you, you have already found us. I am so glad to be found of you! Help others in their search and discovery.

Amen.

—MARJORIE L. KIMBROUGH

Reflecting on her prayer, Marjorie Kimbrough says, "I meet so many young people who are searching for God. I encourage them to keep searching, knowing that they have been found." She is a member of the Cascade United Methodist Church in Atlanta, Georgia, where her husband serves as pastor.

SLEEPING OUT

It is better, I believe, to awaken to
the call of the robin & the wren
When the Sun of Day comes
Than the jangle of big ben & westclock
It is better, I believe,
To be covered with the canopy of stars &
sky & dream
Long forgotten dream, better for me
than a bed of down
As a forest is better than any town,
for living things
& tho men make miracles all the time
The most beautiful are the ones that
ever become the seed of the next one, to be
Like trees & waters & worlds & men
Like love
Like God
Like life is
I believe

—DELBERT TIBBS

Delbert Tibbs is a writer-poet who was born in Mississippi in 1939. He received
his education at South East City College, Chicago State University, and Chicago
Theological Seminary. He presently resides in Chicago, where he has lived for
many years.

FOR FORGIVENESS

LORD, I REPENT

Blessed Lord,

From the bottom of my heart, I pray in deep repentance. My guilt overwhelms me. I have not lived my life according to Your precepts. Your expectations are great and I feel unworthy of Your unconditional love. Your guidance I have not heeded. Help me overcome temptations. Strengthen me where I am weak and build me up where I am torn down. I humbly ask You for Your forgiveness and pray for the strength to make a new beginning. Though I am not worthy, please grant me Your infinite mercy and help me to mature and become more like You. I pray in Christ's Name.

Amen.

—REVEREND CHESTINA MITCHELL ARCHIBALD

Reflecting on this prayer, Reverend Archibald says, "Sin invariably brings hurt and disappointment. There is no protection for sin. Yet, the word of God tells us that 'God sent not His Son into the world to condemn the world, but that the world through Him might be saved'" (John 3:17). Despite the fact that human nature is prone to imperfection, if we ask for God's forgiveness, He will grant it.

A Prayer of Deep Repentance

Dear God,

How can we ever be worthy of Your precious love? You who suffered and died for our iniquities. Yet, Your love is forever with us, and You stand ready to make all things right. We have sinned greatly in the past and all of us fall short of Your glory. We have called ourselves grasshoppers and we have called grasshoppers giants. With these collected sins of all generations on our shoulders, it becomes forever important to stand before You and feel Your love. I wish I could wash away the pain in Your heart. Help us live up to the potential Thou hast placed within us. You have given us gifts and we have buried them. Forgive us, Lord, I pray. Jesus has paid the great price for historical sins and opened the way for the forgiveness of all sins for those who believe in Him. For His great and noble sacrifices I am eternally grateful and rest in the assurance that nothing is impossible with Thee. In His Holy Name I Pray.

    Amen.

—Reverend Chestina Mitchell Archibald

This prayer of Reverend Archibald's was influenced by 2 Chronicles 7:14: "If my people which are called by my name, shall humble themselves and pray, and see my face and turn from their wicked ways: then will I hear from heaven, and will forgive their sins and will heal their land." Because of His unconditional love for us, God pardons the sins of those who repent.

CONFESSION AND REPENTANCE

Merciful One,
seeing our own shortcomings
is hardest
to do
and, not seeing them,
we abused our promise
and strayed from you.

But facing them today,
as a part of coming back,
we seek your pardon.
We part from them now!
Since you know inner hearts
better than we know outer deeds,
you know our repentance
and regret that our conduct
missed the mark.

Help us make amends
through your strength.

—REVEREND WILL E. CHAMBERS

In "Confession and Repentance," the second part of his work *Prayer Portions*, Reverend Chambers reminds us that although we may fail to honor God's will at times, if we ask Him for forgiveness, He will always show us mercy. He has written many articles for his church paper, *The Christian Index*, and has had his poetry published in such publications as *The Winston-Salem Chronicle* and *Piedmont Peddler*.

MERCY

O God, You made us and You know all about us. We cannot hide ourselves from You. If we were to go to the top of the mountain, You would be there. If we were to go the depth of the valley, You would be there also. God, we come to You acknowledging that we are like sheep gone astray. We have failed to honor You with our living and our giving. Have mercy, Lord. We have withheld the truth and stretched the truth. Have mercy, Lord. We have participated and planned acts of deceit and conceit. Have mercy, Lord. We need the forgiveness of our brothers and sisters. Lord, give us the courage to ask for the forgiveness we so desperately need from You. Please Lord, have mercy.

Amen.

—REVEREND YVONNE HOWZE

A graduate of Vanderbilt Divinity School, Reverend Howze has recently become pastor of St. James African Methodist Episcopal Church in Birmingham, Alabama. A wife and mother of three children, she has been a pastor for thirteen years.

FORGIVENESS AND RESTITUTION

Almighty God of Mercy,

I come before You in humble submission, repenting for my sins. Though I sincerely believe in Your forgiveness, I seek to right my wrongs through a form of restitution acceptable to You. I feel that my repentance is simply not enough. I pray to be able to pay back my great debt to You in some way. Lord, I know that the debt is too great to repay in action alone and it is only through the blood of Jesus that we are washed clean and made pure as gold. I know forgiveness flows freely to those who sincerely repent. Please accept my humble repentance as I lay prostrate before Your throne of grace. Lord, please receive my efforts with my heartfelt prayer of gratitude for Your everlasting love and kindness shown us through Your gift to the world, Your only begotten Son, Jesus the Christ. In Christ's Name.

Amen.

—REVEREND CHESTINA MITCHELL ARCHIBALD

Reverend Archibald found inspiration for this prayer in Psalms 103:1–3: "Bless the Lord, O my soul and all that is within me, bless His Holy name, bless the Lord, O my soul, and forget not all his benefits: Who forgiveth all thine iniquities; who healeth all thy diseases." Sincere and humble repentance is enough for God to grant His forgiveness.

HUNGER

When we get up in the morning Lord, we often hunger for food. Forgive us, as we should be hungry for thy word. As our physical being yearns for food, so does our spiritual being hunger and thirst after righteousness. Feed us, nourish us, that our thirst may be satisfied until we are filled to completion.

Amen.

—REVEREND ETELL WASHINGTON

Reverend Etell Washington is a minister at Prince Chapel Missionary Baptist Church in Los Angeles, California. This prayer expresses our continuing need for nourishment from the Word of God.

A Clean Heart and Right Spirit

God of forgiveness, grace, and mercy, to You we humbly bow. We thank You for being a God who does not hold our offenses against us but hears our cries for deliverance. O Lord, we know we have not lived according to Your will; we know we have not loved one another as we should; and we know that we continue to stray from the narrow path of Jesus. We all can give excuses for our disobedience but this only stunts our growth in grace. Lord, forgive us again as You've done in the past. Give us a clean heart and restore a right spirit in us that we may more worthily serve Thee. As you grant us courage, grant us wisdom for the living of these days.

Amen.

—Reverend Chestina Mitchell Archibald

The Lord's Prayer served as inspiration for Reverend Archibald when writing this prayer: "Forgive us our trespasses as we forgive those who trespass against us." In the same way that God shows mercy to us, despite knowing that we have sinned, we must show mercy to others who may have wronged us in some way.

A Prayer on Forgiveness

Lord, I pledge to be forgiving as You have forgiven me. Never let me betray anyone—and if I do, Lord, please help me to say at once that I am sorry. Teach me that You always forgive, no matter what the sin. May I be quick to forgive others. I am reminded that if I do not forgive others, neither will You forgive me, and my soul will remain forever filled with the tense corruption that lack of forgiveness brings.

Amen.

—Reverend Chestina Mitchell Archibald

This prayer was inspired by Matthew 6:14–15: "For if ye forgive men their trespasses, your heavenly Father will also forgive you: But if ye forgive not men their trespasses, neither will your Father forgive your trespasses." We must pray to God for the strength to forgive others, even when they have betrayed us in some way, just as God has mercy on us when we sin against Him.

LORD, CLEANSE MY SPIRIT

O, thou sin-forgiving God, they that are whole need not a physician, but they that are sick. Lord, I am sick, and full of diseases. If thou wilt, thou canst make me clean. Though my sins have been as scarlet, thou canst make them as wool; and though they be red like crimson, thou canst make them whiter than snow. Were it not that there is a sufficiency in thy blood to atone for the vilest, the view of my past sins and transgressions would sink me in despair. But thou hast said, him that cometh to thee, thou wilt in no wise cast out. Lord, I come, pleading alone the merits of my Redeemer; not only for myself do I plead, but for the whole race of mankind; especially for the benighted sons and daughters of Africa. Do thou loose their bonds and let the oppressed go free. Bless thy churches throughout the world. Clothe thy ministers with salvation, and cause thy saints to shout for joy. Grant that the time may soon come, that all may know thee from the rising of the sun unto the going down thereof. In an especial manner wilt thou look down upon the church to which I belong. Fire our souls with a holy zeal for thy cause, and let us not rest at ease in Zion, whilst souls are perishing for the lack of knowledge. Wilt thou increase her number of such, and such only, as shall be saved. Bless our pastor with a double portion of thy Spirit. Encourage his heart, and strengthen him in the inward man, and may he see the work of the Lord prosper in his hands. And now, Lord, what wait I for? Dispel every gloomy fear that pervades my mind, and to thee I will ascribe praises everlasting.

—MARIA W. STEWART (1803–1879)

An early feminist, Maria Stewart published a small pamphlet, *Religion and the Pure Principles of Morality, the Sure Foundation on Which We Must Build,* and in 1832 began an unprecedented public speaking tour in Boston. She was the first woman in the United States to engage in public political debates.

A PRAYER FOR EVENING WORSHIP

O thou King eternal, immortal, invisible, and only wise God, before whom angels bow and seraphs veil their faces, crying, holy, holy, holy, is the Lord God Almighty. True and righteous are thy ways, thou King of saints. Help me, thy poor unworthy creature, humbly to prostrate myself before thee, and implore thou mercy which my sins have justly forfeited. O God, I know that I am not worthy of a place at thy footstool; but to whom shall I go but unto thee? Thou alone hast the words of eternal life. Send me not away without a blessing, I beseech thee; but enable me to wrestle like Jacob, and to prevail like Israel. Be graciously pleased, O God, to pardon all that thou hast seen amiss in me this day, and enable me to live more to thine honor and glory for the time to come. Bless the church to which I belong, and grant that when thou makest up thy jewels, not one soul shall be found missing. Bless him in whom thou hast set over us a watchman in Zion. Let not his soul be discouraged. May he not fail to declare the whole counsel of God, whether sinners will hear or forbear. And now, Lord, what wait I for? My hope is in thee. Do more for me than I can possibly ask or think, and finally receive me to thyself.

—MARIA W. STEWART (1803–1879)

This poem expresses Maria W. Stewart's wishes to be blessed by God and to be forgiven any wrongdoings she may have performed that day. It is a prayer which reminds us that if we listen for God's voice, He will come to us and guide us.

FOR GUIDANCE

I NEED THEE EVERY HOUR

I need thee every hour, most gracious Lord;
No tender voice like thine can peace afford.
I need thee every hour; stay thou near by;
Temptations lose their power when thou art nigh.
I need thee every hour, in joy or pain;
Come quickly and abide, or life is vain.
I need thee every hour; teach me thy will;
And thy rich promises in me fulfill.
I need thee, O I need thee,
Every hour I need thee;
O bless me now, my Savior,
I come to Thee!

—ANNIE S. HAWKS (1835–1918)

A longtime resident of Brooklyn, New York, Annie S. Hawks was a writer of religious songs. "I Need Thee Every Hour" is her best-known hymn. Written in 1872, it first appeared in a small collection prepared for the National Baptist Sunday School Association.

STAND BY ME

When the storms of life are raging,
Stand by me;
When the storms of life are raging,
Stand by me.
When the world is tossing me,
like a ship upon the sea;
Thou who rulest wind and water,
Stand by me.

In the midst of tribulation,
Stand by me;
In the midst of tribulation,
Stand by me.
When the hosts of hell assail,
And my strength begins to fail,
Thou who never lost a battle,
Stand by me.

In the midst of faults and failures,
Stand by me;
In the midst of faults and failures,
Stand by me.
When I do the best I can,
And my friends misunderstand,
Thou who knowest all about me,
Stand by me.

In the midst of persecution,
Stand by me;
In the midst of persecution,
Stand by me.

When my foes in battle array
Undertake to stop my way,
Thou who saved Paul and Silas,
Stand by me.

When I'm growing old and feeble,
Stand by me;
When I'm growing old and feeble,
Stand by me.
When my life becomes a burden,
And I'm nearing chilly Jordan,
O Thou "Lily of the Valley,"
Stand by me.

—CHARLES ALBERT TINDLEY (1851–1933)

Charles Albert Tindley's *New Songs of Paradise*, published in 1916, was the first collection of spirituals by a black songwriter. Tindley began as a preacher who sang at religious camp meetings and eventually settled in Philadelphia, where he founded the East Calvary Methodist Episcopal Church in 1902. Although Thomas Andrew Dorsey is sometimes referred to as the first gospel composer, it was actually Tindley who inspired Dorsey (during a performance of his spiritual "I Do, Don't You" at a National Baptist Convention) to leave popular music and start writing gospel songs.

MY STEADFAST SHELTER

How comforted I am to come into Your house, dear Lord. Your house is everywhere You can find an object of Your outreaching love. No matter where I am, God, I know You prepare a haven for me so I feel safe and secure in the cradle of Your care. Yea, though I walk through the valley of death, You protect me always in Your steadfast shelter. Lord, I pray for all people to reach the point in their lives where they will reach out to You in prayer to begin the one relationship which will truly change their lives and affect their eternal destinies. Please bless now and guide me always as I run this eternal race. In Christ's Name.

Amen.

—REVEREND CHESTINA MITCHELL ARCHIBALD

Unwavering faith brings great comfort and reassurance. On this theme, Reverend Archibald is inspired by the words of the traditional hymn: "O God, my help in ages past, my hope for years to come, my shelter from the stormy blast, and my eternal home."

A Prayer

'Mid the discordant noises of the day I hear thee calling;
I stumble as I fare along earth's way; keep me from falling.

Mine eyes are open, but they cannot see for gloom of night;
I can no more than lift my heart to thee for inward light.

The wild and fiery passion of my youth consumes my soul;
In agony I turn to thee for truth and self-control.

For Passion and all the pleasures it can give will die the death;
But this of me eternally must live, thy borrowed breath.

'Mid the discordant noises of the day I hear thee calling;
I stumble as I fare along earth's way; keep me from falling.

—CLAUDE MCKAY (1890–1948)

Born in Jamaica, Claude McKay had published two books of verse by the time he was twenty-three. After receiving an award from the Jamaica Institute of Arts and Sciences, he was able to study at Tuskegee Institute and Kansas State. He later moved to New York City, where he became a prominent figure in the Harlem Renaissance.

PRECIOUS LORD, TAKE MY HAND

Precious Lord, take my hand,
Lead me on, let me stand,
I am tired, I am weak, I am worn
Thru the storm, thru the night,
Lead me on to the light,
Take my hand, precious Lord,
Lead me home.

When my way grows drear, precious Lord, linger near,
When my life is almost gone,
Hear my cry, hear my call,
Hold my hand lest I fall;
Take my hand, precious Lord,
Lead me home.

When the darkness appears and the night draws near,
And the day is past and gone,
At the river I stand,
Guide my feet, hold my hand;
Take my hand, precious Lord,
Lead me home.

—THOMAS ANDREW DORSEY (1899–1993)

Born near Atlanta, Georgia, Thomas Andrew Dorsey is considered the foremost composer of gospel music. He started out playing blues piano in saloons in Chicago, under the name "Georgia Tom," until he saw Charles Albert Tindley perform at a National Baptist Convention. Dorsey then devoted himself to writing songs with religious themes, writing over 1,000 gospel songs before his death. This, his best-known hymn (made famous by Mahalia Jackson), was inspired by the tragic loss he suffered when his wife died during childbirth and their baby passed away a day later.

Guide Me in Your Word

God, be my guide in all my understanding. Help me to see the best in all I see. Guide my mouth that I may speak words of kindness. Guide my heart that I may share Your love. Open my eyes that I may see Your truth and my hands that I may give freely in Your name. Teach me O God, my King, to do everything as though it were for You.

Give me the courage I need O God to endure temptation. Guide me in my period of tribulation. When evil seeks to destroy me, come to my aid. When wrath is upon me, lead me out. When I face the gates of death, loving Savior be on my side. I love You, be forever my guide.

Lord my guide and strength, be my guide when I face death or in life.
When I face falsehood or truth.
When I face despair or hope.
When I face fear or trust.
When I face hatred or love.
When I face war or peace.
In this world I will face tribulations, but I am of good courage, because You have overcome the world. In Your Holy Name, Amen.

—Reverend Chestina Mitchell Archibald

The inspiration for this prayer was found in Deuteronomy 31:6: "Be strong and of good courage, fear not, nor be afraid . . . for the Lord thy God . . . doth go with thee; he will not fail thee, nor forsake thee." God's gifts of strength, guidance, and courage can help us to overcome any obstacle we may encounter along the way.

HELP ME MAKE WORTHY DECISIONS, LORD

Lord,

Help me make up my mind swiftly and with divine inspiration. I do not want to waste time and anguish over decisions I must make, so I ask You to sharpen my decision making ability. I pray that my decisions be centered on You and not self-serving. At crossroads, each direction seems like a good course to take. You have given us a free will, but we need Your divine guidance. When I cannot decide which road to take, please give me the gift of discernment to know Your will. Make Your will clear to me. Always guide my decisions. In moments of indecision may I always pause until Your will is clear and may I always have the courage to take the road less traveled. I pray this in Christ's Name.

   Amen.

—REVEREND CHESTINA MITCHELL ARCHIBALD

Reverend Archibald cites Joel 3:14b as an influence in the writing of this prayer: "For the day of the Lord is near in the valley of decision." Although God has given us free will, if we remain open to His direction, He will aid us in making the right decisions.

FACING LIFE'S EXAMS

O Lord, as we prepare to face Life's final exam, help us to pass the exam for God, which asks those of us being examined to make certain choices: whether or not to feed the poor; to give drink to the thirsty; to befriend the strangers; to clothe the naked; to heal the sick; to befriend the prisoner. Lord, who said that life was a series of meaningless choices? And who can say that the evidence Christ will look for at his return is not the same evidence he wants to see in believers today? To love Jesus is to love all who need our care.

As we depart, may the grace of God Almighty comfort us, may the shouts of joy and freedom's echo from our foreparents drive us on toward our hallowed place. Help us to mount our chariots of righteousness and happiness destined for freedom's lane. May those who follow from within these hallowed walls fall in the footsteps of those saints of blackness who gave their full measure of devotion for us all.

Let us truly sing, my country 'tis of thee, sweet land of liberty of thee we sing, land where my fathers and mothers died, land of the African pride, from every mountainside, let freedom ring. Thank God Almighty now freedom rings, peace at last, thank God Almighty for giving us peace at last.

    Amen.

—REVEREND PAUL H. EASLEY

Reverend Easley is campus minister at Clark University in Atlanta, Georgia. Commenting on the theme of his prayer, he says: "It is a challenge to students to face issues in life that confront them."

A PRAYER FOR GUIDANCE

Our Father, our God, we thank you for this moment of sharing, we thank you for your spirit. Lord, we ask now that you bless our debtors. We ask, knowing that you are the architect and the builder, Lord, knowing that you can do all things, we ask now to give us a vision to build. Give us the vision in our hearts and minds. Bless the people with a vision, because we know you said that without a vision we would perish. Give us that vision to see your promise that only you can give.

Now, Lord, we ask these prayers in Jesus' name, and we thank you right now for hearing our prayers, and we know that you've already answered our prayers. In the name of Jesus,

Amen.

—REVEREND JOHNNY GRIMES

Reverend Grimes is currently serving at the New Metropolitan MB Church in Nashville, Tennessee. His prayer reflects the need we all feel to make the right decisions, looking for God's guidance to show us the way.

A PRAYER FOR NEW BEGINNINGS

As I enter into this new endeavor, I am confident that You will be there. You were with me when I was formed in my mama's womb, You have been my shield through good times and bad times. Therefore, I am now ready to undertake this new task, assured of Your ever guiding presence. I don't feel no ways tired, I've come too far from where I started. Nobody told me that the road would be easy. But they told me that if I hold to Your unchanging hand—no matter what I am doing or where I'm sent—everything will be okay. Thank You Lord for this new beginning.

Amen.

—Reverend Chestina Mitchell Archibald

This prayer was based on Psalms 111:10: "The fear of the Lord is the beginning of wisdom: a good understanding have all they that do his commandments: his praise endureth for ever." No matter where we go or what we do, God is, was, and always will be there for us.

I LET GO OF MY ACCUMULATIONS

My ego is like a fortress.
I have built its walls stone by stone
To hold out the invasion of the love of God.
But I have stayed here long enough. There is light
Over the barriers. O My God—
The darkness of my house forgive
And overtake my soul.
I relax the barriers.
I abandon all that I think I am,
All that I hope to be,
All that I believe I possess.
I let go of the past,
I withdraw my grasping hand from the future,
And in the great silence of this moment,
I alertly rest my soul.
As the sea gull lays in the wind current,
So I lay myself in the spirit of God.
My dearest human relationships,
My most precious dreams,
I surrender to His care.
All that I have called my own
I give back. All my favorite things
Which I would withhold in my storehouse
From his fearful tyranny,
I let go.
I give myself
Unto Thee, O my God.
    Amen.

—HOWARD THURMAN (1900–1981)

Howard Thurman was an acclaimed theologian and religious leader. In addition to his many accomplishments, he was dean emeritus of Marsh Chapel at Boston University, and chairman of the Howard Thurman Educational Trust in San Francisco.

ANOINTING

The anointing is the call of God on the life of a person and is evident by the manifestation of the presence of God in the life and work of the individual. One will become the anointed of God by seeking the will of God.

God, I stand in perfect obedience to thy will. It is my desire to be used of you, to be a witness to the world of your son Jesus the Christ. God, I pray that you will give me the anointing that I may be a witness that I will only bring glory to you.

    Amen.

—REVEREND GEORGE S. JENKINS

Reverend Jenkins currently serves at Nehemiah Ministries in North Charleston, South Carolina. His prayer reminds us that the Holy Spirit can come to each of us, allowing God to work through us and make us holy—we merely need to listen for His call.

A PRAYER FOR THE RENEWAL OF FAITH

Heavenly God of the Universe, there are those among us who say that you are dead because you no longer seem to care for us. O Lord, help those who cannot see you to see your marvelous works in the lives of your children. Help them to see your healing power and virtue in once sick bodies. Help them to see your splendid love in the eyes of a once wayward sinner. Help them to see your care for abandoned children through the care of adoptive parents. Help them to see the continued grace of your creation through the kindness of your sunshine, blessing the just and the unjust. Open their eyes that they might see thee and know that you are alive. In the name of thy Son who dies for mankind.

Amen.

—REVEREND H. CARLYLE CHURCH, JR.

Reverend Church received his master of divinity degree from the Howard University School of Divinity in Washington, D.C. He has been the recipient of many awards and honors, including a Citation of Honor by the black caucus of the Oklahoma state legislature and the Thomas A. and Affie M. Wright Fellowship from the Howard University School of Divinity.

A Prayer for One Who Is Single

Lord, I am single and have learned to be content in this state. As a matter of fact, I've become quite happy. I am afraid to bring another into my space, because each time I have done so, it has brought much hurt and disappointment. Now, Lord, I come before Thee who knows my history and who knows my heart, to lead me and guide me in the area of relationships. If I am to have intimate companionship with one other than Thee, make it plain, so that I may no longer stumble in this way. If I am to remain alone, continue to satisfy my soul and steady my mind. Either way, Lord, I will be happy to do Thy will. In the precious name of Your darling son Jesus, who found complete satisfaction in Thee, I pray.

Amen.

—Reverend Chestina Mitchell Archibald

This prayer is based on the following two quotes from the Bible: "I say therefore to the unmarried and widows, it is good for them if they abide even as I am [single]. But if they cannot contain, let them marry: for it is better to marry than to burn" (I Corinthians 7:8–9). "To avoid fornication, let every man have his own wife, and let every woman have her own husband" (I Corinthians 7:2).

UPHOLD US IN YOUR NAME

Almighty God, thanks that there is a strong, bold force of Your holy power on earth. Your heavenly standards shape our lives and fulfill our destinies, though evil forces infiltrate our society, breaking down the moral fabric which binds us. Many insist that Christianity is not different from any other form of religion and should not be the center of our society, yet it is You, through Christ, who has richly blessed this land. Christ is never outdated. May all feel His power and might. Protect our nation. May we never turn our backs on You who have blessed us so richly. May we never neglect to uphold the holy significance of Christ who gave His life for the sake of humanity. Stay here and continue to bless this country. Please, Lord, forgive those who speak and act against You, for they do not know what they are doing. Please accept the repentance of those of us who follow You and attempt to turn from our own wicked ways. Please fortify our hearts and use us as examples of love in the world. Lord, open us to be receptive of a broader understanding of Your truth for we know all people everywhere are Your children. In Christ's Name. Amen.

—REVEREND CHESTINA MITCHELL ARCHIBALD

The motivation behind this prayer came from Psalms 37:27–28: "Depart from evil, and do good; and dwell forevermore. For the Lord loveth judgment, and forsaketh not his saints; they are preserved for ever: but the seed of the wicked shall be cut off." This prayer demonstrates how an undying belief in God can provide the strength to fend off any evils we may encounter.

FOR HEALING

A PRAYER FOR THE HEALING OF THE BODY

Dear Heavenly Father,
Maker of all things great and small,
Maker and master of humanity.
We come as empty vessels,
Seeking to be filled with your
Divine guidance in our time
Of physical weakness and distress.
We ask for the knowledge of the
Healing of our bodies
We know that knowledge is healing
And healing is knowledge.
As we seek knowledge
We ask that you would help us
To find and use this knowledge
to become stronger in our mission
To serve humanity in the name
Of our Lord and Savior Jesus Christ.
We thank you, dear Father,
For we know that you can,
And we know that you will answer prayer.
    Amen.

—REVEREND LILLIE KATE BENITEZ

Reverend Benitez has been active in the arts, particularly poetry, throughout her life. She currently integrates her interest in the humanities with her religious life at Outreach Ministry and the Arts for Children in Atlanta, Georgia.

THE HEALING POWER OF THE LORD

Lord God, many are sick in the land. Touch them with your power of healing. You have all power in your hands and more medicine than all the drug stores in the world. Pour out your Spirit as we reach out to you and accept your healing and affirm your goodness, in Jesus Christ's name we pray.

Amen.

—REVEREND CHARLES W. WILLIAMS

Reverend Williams is the minister of the Christ Centered Missionary Baptist Church in Compton, Missouri. He finds his inspiration for this prayer in the reassuring verse "Thy Word is a lamp unto my feet and a light unto my path" (Psalms 119:105).

A PRAYER FOR HEALING AND COMFORT

Almighty God, our Heavenly Father, it's in a state of obedient humbleness and with a reliance and dependence that I come before thy throne of grace and thy throne of mercy. I first and foremost give thee thanks from the tip of my tongue to the depth of my heart and soul for your continued blessing. I give thee thanks for the privilege you've afforded me to spiritually communicate with thee, and to strengthen such a meaningful relationship. I wish to take this opportunity, my Father, to pray for not only myself but more so for others less fortunate than myself. Persons suffering from the plague, diseases, addictions, and various kinds of mental and physical illnesses. I pray for healing, my Father, in the name of Jesus, for I know the power is in His name. For those persons in agony, pain, and grief, I ask you, my Father, to have compassion and allow Jesus to be the comforter you promised you would send. Have mercy upon our souls, Lord, and forgive us for our committed sins. Teach us your ways and direct us in your path. Protect us from all harms, danger, and from our enemies, particularly those who plot secretly against us. Teach us to love not only ourselves but one another, for it's in the name of Jesus I pray.

Amen.

—REVEREND ALFONSO T. DELANEY

Presently serving at the Ebenezer United Methodist Church in Miami, Florida, Reverend Delaney is also a licensed pastoral counselor, pastoral clinical counselor, and Christian clinical therapist. He is currently pursuing a Ph.D. in theocentric psychology at Lasalle University.

A HOLISTIC PRAYER

God, I come today to thank You for holism and healing of my mind body and spirit. You have wrapped my wounds and a scab of protection has formed. May I forever be mindful that the protective scab will fall as memory of past hurts fades and complete forgiveness takes place. Thank You Lord for continued growth as I strive towards perfection in Thee.

    Amen.

—REVEREND CHESTINA MITCHELL ARCHIBALD

In writing this prayer, Reverend Archibald was inspired by Hebrews 6:I: "Therefore, leaving the principles of the doctrine of Christ, let us go on unto perfection. . . ." The prayer illustrates how God's love can help us to heal ourselves.

PRAYER OF HEALING

Almighty and Eternal Father,
In whose law is our life,
And whose mercy is everlasting,
We come as humble as we know how,
Asking for healing of our
Minds, bodies and souls.

We come in great faith that
In your word you did say, "Ask,
And it shall be given,
Seek, and ye shall find, knock,
And the door will be open."
We ask in the precious name
Of Jesus that you would grant
Us Healing of the mind,
That we might glorify and
Give witness to the unlimited
Love and Blessings received
Each day of our lives.

We thank you, dear Father, we know
That you can and we know
That you will.

—REVEREND LILLIE KATE BENITEZ

Finding inspiration to write this prayer in Matthew 7:7–8, Reverend Benitez says: "Whenever I ask God for something, it is always given to me in his own time. Whenever I seek information, knowledge, or a solution to a problem, I always find answers. And finally, when I'm confronted with a trying solution, I work hard, put forth as much effort as I can, and seek God's help to overcome obstacles."

ALMIGHTY, DIVINE, INFINITE SPIRIT WITHIN ME IS HEALING ME NOW

There is no incurable disease. Erroneous thoughts produce disease. Positive thoughts move and build the body. Whenever I speak, I cause the atoms in my body to change places, as well as lower or raise the vibrations that affect my body. I now release from my mind all unforgiving thoughts. I forgive myself for all the mistakes I have made. I forgive others who seemed to hurt me in any way. To forgive is to love. I love myself and give others the freedom to be. I admit that of myself, I am powerless to solve any problem.

The Almighty, Divine, Infinite Spirit within me is now pulsating, restoring, renewing and revitalizing my immune system, every organ, cell, tissue and atom of my being. My blood stream is cleansed. I feel this; I believe it; I accept it and give thanks for it. Thank you, Father.

—REVEREND CARMEN YOUNG

A resident of Pinelake, Georgia, Reverend Young says: "I love to write things to help people." Reverend Young currently works at Divine Truth Ministries, a nondenominational organization, where she teaches motivational classes on topics such as improving relationships, how to become successful, and dealing with emotional problems. The organization has held annual conferences since 1995, as well as various workshops and services.

FOR STRENGTH

A Prayer for Strength

Eternal God, Creator of heaven and earth, I thank thee for allowing me to assemble in your presence. I give thee praise and exhort your holy name. As I cry out my soul to thee, hear my cry of desperation. Lift up the heavy burden from my shoulders so that I might stand erect, may weaknesses be changed into strengths, and may the obstacles be removed from my path. Transform me from darkness into the light of Jesus as I seek the gift of salvation. May I be lifted up above the oppressions and depressions of life as I pray for the closeness to thee in my heart. In the name of Jesus.

Amen.

—Reverend Alfonso T. Delaney

In addition to pastoring, Reverend Delaney is the national alumni chaplain for Bethune-Cookman College in Daytona Beach, Florida. He received his B.A. degree from Bethune-Cookman College, and his master of divinity degree from the International Theological Center in Atlanta, Georgia.

A PRAYER FOR GUIDANCE

O Lord who has shown Yourself to be just and fair, we uplift Your holy name. We thank You for guiding and directing our lives. We thank You for Your commandments and our ordinances. For we know that if we learn to do Your will—if we learn to live how You called us to live—then Your kingdom will begin to come forth here on earth. O Lord, we only ask that in our daily walks of life, as we go from day to day interacting with one another, that Your Holy Spirit moves in such a way that it remains in the forefront of our minds. O Lord, help us as we strive to have lifestyles that are pleasing in Your eyes. In the name of Jesus, in Whose footsteps we desire to walk, we pray.

Amen.

—REVEREND CHESTINA MITCHELL ARCHIBALD

Reverend Archibald was motivated by Psalms 37:5 in the writing of this prayer: "Commit thy way unto the Lord; trust also in him; and he shall bring it to pass." If we continue to follow the direction God has given us, He will lead us straight to His Kingdom.

LET GO OF EVERYTHING BUT GOD

I must let go.
For so long I have held the habit of holding on. Even my muscles
Are tense; deeply fearful are they
Of relaxing lest they fall away from their place.
I cling clutchingly to my friends
Lest I lose them.
I live under the shadow of being supplanted by another.

I cling to my money, not so much
By a wise economy and a thoughtful spending
But by a sense of possession that makes me depend upon it for
    strength.
I must let go—
deep at the core of me
I must have the sense of freedom—
A sure awareness of detachment—
of relaxation.

I must let go of everything.
I must let go of pride. But—
What am I saying? Is there not a sense of pride
That supports and sustains all achievement,
Even the essential dignity of my own personality?
It may be that I must let go
My dependence upon triumphing over my fellows,
which seems
To give me a sense of security in their midst.
I cringe from my pain; I do not relish
The struggle of life but I do not want to let go

Because the hurt and the tension of contest feed
The springs of my pride. They make me deeply aware.
But I must let go of everything.
I must let go of everything but God.
But God—May it not be
That God is in all the things to which I cling?
That may be the hidden reason for my clinging.
It is all very puzzling indeed. When I say
I must "let go of everything but God"
What is my meaning?
I must relax my hold on everything that dulls my sense of Him,
That comes between me and the inner awareness of His Presence
Pervading my life and glorifying
All the common ways with wonderful wonder.

"Teach me, O God, how to free myself of dearest possessions,
So that in my trust I shall find restored to me
All I need to walk in Thy path and to fulfill Thy will.
Let me know Thee for myself that I may not be satisfied
With aught that is less."

—HOWARD THURMAN (1900–1981)

One of Howard Thurman's greatest achievements as an outstanding religious leader was guiding a delegation of black Christians to Asia, where they met with the members of the Student Christian Movement in India, Burma, and Ceylon in 1935.

A PRAYER FOR SPIRITUAL RENEWAL

Spirit of the Living God, fall afresh on me. Spirit of the Living God, fall afresh on me. Mold me, make me. Spirit of the Living God, fall afresh on me. Lord, You are the great teacher, there is none greater than You. You give us tasks and then allow us to be attacked by all manner of difficulties. Yet, as we scramble to fulfill our responsibilities and overcome these difficulties, our faith deepens as we begin to embody a sincere understanding of Your existence and how we must rely on You. Life is the training ground for our spiritual growth, and You are our Master. Let us be mindful of life's lessons and prepare our spirit through this training in order that we might be able to live with You and dwell with You in Your kingdom when we leave this earth. In Christ's Name.

Amen.

—REVEREND CHESTINA MITCHELL ARCHIBALD

Psalms 51:10 highlights the theme of this prayer: "Create in me a clean heart, O God; and renew a right spirit within me." Reliance on God allows us to conquer life's hurdles as we gain a deeper understanding of our spirituality.

A TRADITIONAL PRAYER

Most Holy and all wise God Our Heavenly Father, a few of your believing children have bowed at this your house one time more. We didn't come for no shape form of fashion neither for an outside show to this dying world, but we come this morning because we didn't know nobody that could do our needy soul any good but you and you alone. Before I go any farther into prayer: I want to thank you for my last night's lying down and this morning's early rising. Lord, when I rose this morning I found I was still in the land of the living, voice wasn't hushed up in death, footsteps weren't silent to be heard no more in the land, garments were not my shroud, my bed was not my cooling board. I was able to move and still have my being in this your world. Lord, thank you for my neighbors and bless my neighbors' children. Go with us and stand by us a few days longer. Master, lead us and we will be led, guide us, and we won't go wrong. Bless this world at large. After you have blessed this whole round world please remember this your poor weak and humble servant. I'm no ways worried, no ways tired of trying to suit and to serve you. Strengthen me where I'm so weak and build me up where I'm all torn down. Be a leaning post in these times of trouble. Now Lord, when I have wound up my last ball of trouble, gone in my room never to come out no more, give me an easy coasting death, a happy hour in a changed world where I can be with you in peace. In Jesus' name, I ask it all.

Amen.

—ANNIE DOUGLAS

Annie Douglas is a member of the Mount Olivet Baptist Church. Residing in a remote part of Hendersonville, Tennessee, she acts as the archivist for the area.

PRAYER FOR REVITALIZATION

Although the day is not nearly over, a great weariness has descended on me. I feel it is not a physical weariness, but a weariness of spirit. I feel drained and in need of revitalization. I pray with a burdened heart, O Lord, and beg You to fill my weary soul with Your divine breath of life. Let the sweetness of Your love flow into my tired spirit and revive me to do Your bidding. In Christ's Name.

Amen.

—REVEREND CHESTINA MITCHELL ARCHIBALD

Inspiration for this prayer came from Isaiah 40:31: "But they that wait upon the Lord shall renew their strength; they shall mount up with wings as eagles; they shall run, and not be weary; and they shall walk, and not faint." The prayer describes the spiritual weariness we all feel sometimes, and how if we ask for God's help, He can revive us with His love.

AN EVENING PRAYER

Father, we call Thee "Father" because we love Thee. We are glad to be called Thy children, and to dedicate our lives to the service that extends through willing hearts and hands to the betterment of all mankind. We send up our cry of Thanksgiving for people of all races, creeds, classes and colors, the world over, and pray that through the instrumentality of our lives, the spirit of peace, joy, fellowship and brotherhood shall belt the world.

We know that this world is filled with discordant notes, but help us, Father, to so unite our efforts that we may all join in one harmonious symphony for peace and brotherhood, justice and equality of opportunity for all men.

The tasks performed today with forgiveness for all our errors, we dedicate, Dear Lord, to Thee. Grant us strength and courage and faith and humility sufficient for the tasks assigned to us.

Amen.

—MARY MCLEOD BETHUNE (1875–1955)

Born to South Carolina sharecroppers, Mary McLeod Bethune stepped off a train in Daytona Beach, Florida, in 1902 with only $1.50, her son, and the desire to open a school for black children. By 1923, the small school she had built on the former city dump had become Bethune College, which later merged with Cookman College to become Bethune-Cookman College, still in existence.

A NOTE TO NOTICE

Be
& Be not deceived by the ways of men
& beings. Be quick & silent
See & be not dismayed. For indeed
God is not mocked, nor true seekers of
His ways.
Cast fear away but stay, always within
the ways of appropriateness which some
call "The Way"
Friends and relatives & the closest kin
will willfully—sometimes, bad, wrong,
& sometimes for ignorance and ways not
understood—will see the great good
but be wrong.
The Supreme Self, Lord of the worlds, is
the only hold
& will make strong. Be tolerant & long
on understanding and unequivocal in the way. All times.
All ways. Everywhere.
Night & days.
For all . . . all, are the Lord's.
Yes.

—DELBERT TIBBS

In Florida in 1974, Delbert Tibbs was arrested and charged with rape and murder. Although he maintained that he was innocent, he was found guilty and sentenced to death. Three years later, after a massive nationwide campaign for his life, spearheaded by the Delbert Tibbs Defense Committee, the Florida High Court overturned the sentence. Despite his ordeal, his faith in God never wavered, as exemplified in this prayer from his book *Poems, Prayers, & Logics.*

A PRAYER ON SELF-WORTH

I am somebody.
I may be poor,

                    but I am somebody.

I may be uneducated,
I may be unskilled,

                    but I am somebody.

I may be on welfare,
I may be prematurely pregnant,
I may be on drugs,
I may be victimized by racism,

                    but I am somebody.

Respect me. Protect me. Never neglect me.
I am God's child.

—REVEREND JESSE L. JACKSON

Born in South Carolina in 1941, Jesse Jackson has become one of the most accomplished political activists of the twentieth century. He began his full-time involvement with the civil rights movement in 1965, and also assisted Martin Luther King, Jr., with the Southern Christian Leadership Conference (SCLC). In addition to being founder-president of the National Rainbow Coalition, a national social justice organization devoted to empowerment, education, and mobilization, he was a U.S. presidential candidate in 1984 and 1988, and in 1990 was elected to the U.S. Senate from Washington, D.C., as a "Shadow Senator" without voting rights. This prayer was taken from Reverend Jackson's book *Straight from the Heart.*

SPIRITUALS

Rocks and the firm roots of trees.
The rising shafts of mountains.
Something strong to put my hands on.

Sing, O Lord Jesus!
Song is a strong thing.
I heard my mother singing
When life hurt her:

Gonna ride in my chariot some day!

The branches rise
From the firm roots of trees.
The mountains rise
From the solid lap of earth.
The waves rise
From the dead weight of sea.

Sing, O black mother!
Song is a strong thing.

—LANGSTON HUGHES (1902–1967)

Born in 1902 in Joplin, Missouri, Langston Hughes has become one of the most influential and prolific black poets in history. His first volume of poetry, *The Weary Blues*, was published in 1926, and he soon became part of the Harlem Renaissance movement. As a result of his talent, he was awarded a scholarship at Lincoln University in Pennsylvania, as well as a Guggenheim Fellowship in 1935 and a Rosenwald Fellowship in 1940. During his lifetime, he devoted himself to writing not only poetry, but also short stories, essays, plays, humor, lyrics, and an autobiography.

QUIETNESS AND CONFIDENCE

"In quietness and confidence shall be your strength."
Long before I was born God was at work
Creating life, nature and the world of men and things.
The worlds were ideas in the mind of God
That have been realizing themselves through the ages.
God is not through with creation—
God is not through with me.
In quietness and confidence shall be my strength
"Acquaint now thyself with him and be at peace."
In many ways I am getting acquainted with myself.
Always I seek a deeper understanding of my true self—
The very core of me.
What I would be and am not yet, reassures me.
Through my innermost self I find my way to God.
I shall acquaint myself with him and be at peace.
"I will fly in the greatness of God as the marsh hen flies,
Filling all the space twixt the marsh and the skies."
What I seek beyond is what I am finding within.
The beyond is within.
The signature of God is all around me
In the rocks, in the trees, in the minds of men.
"I will fly in the greatness of God as the marsh hen flies."
"I will fear no evil; for Thou art with me."
I can never be overcome by evil
Until the evil that threatens
Moves from without
within.

This does not mean that I shall not be hurt by evil,
Shall not be frustrated by evil,
That I shall say evil is not evil.
I shall see the travail of my own life with evil
And be unafraid.
For "Thou art with me;
Thy rod and Thy staff, they all comfort me."

—HOWARD THURMAN (1900–1981)

Howard Thurman, a graduate of Morehouse College, received national recognition as a preacher. He also published *Jesus and the Disinherited*, which illustrates how the Gospel may be used as a manual for those going through difficult times.

A PRAYER AGAINST NEGATIVITY

O Lord, we praise Your Holy Name. We are thankful that in Your omnipotence we are not too insignificant to merit Your attention. We know our limitations, our faults, and our weaknesses but in that knowledge we shout hallelujah because we also know we can do all things as You strengthen us. O Lord, we ask that You deliver us from negativity, but when faced with a mountain give us strength to climb. Help us to claim and teach others to claim tomorrow's victory with today's faith. Help us to trust You for You are trustworthy. We know the one who doubts should not expect anything from You so cleanse us of doubt so that we may be freed for joyful obedience. We say thank You again for all You have done, are doing, and we know by faith will do in the future. In Jesus' name we pray.

Amen.

—REVEREND CHESTINA MITCHELL ARCHIBALD

Motivation for writing this prayer was prompted by Philippians 4:13: "I can do all things through Christ that strengthens me." In a world where it is often difficult to trust or rely on others, we know that God will always be there for us, showing us the way with His love.

A Prayer for Self-Image

Please excuse me, Lord, for having accepted these perverted images that others set as standards. Thank You for giving me plenty of good food to eat and good health and good looks. I spend much time dwelling on my weight and being unhappy with the shape of my body. Society has created an image of beauty which is foolish. Most folk honestly want to be big in the legs, little in the waist, and sweet in the face, to have plenty of sense, and the Holy Ghost too. But without You, Lord, there is no beauty. The hearts of fallen humankind are far from Yours, but I pray for people to find You, O God, and to heal their undernourished souls. I pray to be able to truly transcend the power of my misguided ego and the desire to please the misguided egos of others. I pray to place my values in You and what is Yours, not on where society is placing ever-changing values. Forgive me for allowing myself to be sucked into the self-centered world of those who look only at external things, forgetting things which are internal. God, from now on, I ask You to liberate me from worrying about the sickness of this world. Please guide my mind and heart with Your own. In Christ's Name.

Amen.

—Reverend Chestina Mitchell Archibald

The theme of this prayer is illustrated in Psalms 149:4: "For the Lord taketh pleasure in His people: He will beautify the meek with salvation." In today's society, it is easy to get caught up in shallow standards of what is beautiful—but those who know God realize that the truly important values are those which beautify on the inside.

A PRAYER FOR DETERMINATION

In these first beginnings of the new life in the world, renew us in the resolution to persist in the good work we have begun. Give us strength of body and strength of mind and the unfaltering determination to carry out that which we know to be good and right.

Forgive all wavering in the past service of Thy cause and make us strong to go forward in spite of the doubts of our friends and our enemies and in spite of our own distrust in ourselves. Out of the death of winter comes ever and again the resurrection of spring: so out of evil bring good, O God, and out of doubt, determination.

Amen.

—W. E. B. DU BOIS (1868–1963)

A recipient of numerous prestigious honors, W. E. B. Du Bois was awarded the Spingarn Medal by the NAACP in 1920 for founding the Pan-African Congress. During his illustrious career, he lectured on many tours across the United States and England, speaking out on the unjust treatment of blacks and helping to spread the civil rights movement.

GOD, GRANT ME DETERMINATION

Most merciful God, strengthen my will so that I can make decisions and stick to them. Show me the things that really matter and help me to use my energies in the best possible way to accomplish them. Give me the faith to have the assurance of things hoped for and knowledge of things not seen. Grant me the ability to focus on a specific goal or task, and the fortitude and determination to remain steadfast until my dream becomes a reality.

Amen.

—REVEREND CHESTINA MITCHELL ARCHIBALD

The foundation for this prayer comes from Philippians 4:13: "I can do all things through Christ which strengthens me." With God's help to grant determination, confidence, and concentration, any goal can become a reality.

A Prayer of Success

To you, dear Father, who are
The beginning and the end,
King of kings, Savior, Lord,
And our God,
We have confidence that if we
Follow your commandments,
You will place us on a rock
That is higher than high,
That if we study (Ask) your word,
Live by your word (Seek),
And follow your word (Knock),
All doors of opportunities, success,
And salvation will be ours forever.
Strengthen us mentally, physically and spiritually.
We thank you, dear Father,
We know that you can and
We know that you will.
This we pray in the name of
The Father, Son and Holy Spirit.

—Reverend Lillie Kate Benitez

Among her numerous activities and achievements, Reverend Benitez has been a producer for numerous children's plays and has had casting experience for other theatrical works. Active in the arts, she has supplemented her talent for writing with an interest in acting, appearing in several films and commercials.

A PRAYER OF RESTORATION

The Supreme Being! The God of the Universe! The Holy One!

We come seeking your Divine Knowledge and Eternal Widsom. We come beseeching your Magnificent Presence and Infinite Power.

Now, God, we bring our cares and concerns to You. Divorce has become a natural occurrence. Teenage pregnancy has become a common incidence. And crime has become an ordinary episode.

In the midst of this chaos and confusion, we need Your Peace. In the midst of this moral decline and values redefined, we need Your Grace. In the midst of this violence and viciousness, we need Your Mercy.

Spirit of the Living God, indwell us and fill us with Your Love.
   Amen!

—REVEREND KENNETH L. MORRIS

Reverend Morris is a minister in Atlanta, Georgia. His prayer demonstrates the importance of expressing praise and devotion to God, despite our worldly concerns and fears. Once we have acknowledged His power and strength, we will feel stronger and calmer for having put our faith in Him—and our worries in His hands.

FOR HELP TO FOLLOW HIS WILL

A LIGHT UNTO MY FEET AND A LAMP UNTO MY PATH

Jesus spoke to the leaders of His time and scolded them, saying they spent too much time searching the scriptures, attempting to find life, yet the scriptures bore witness to Jesus, who stood before them. They continued to search the scriptures for life but it was He who came to give them life. So concerned were they with the laws of Moses that they were unable to recognize and refused to go to the one who was sent to fulfill the scriptures. Let us be aware, dear Lord, lest we become too caught up in doctrine that we miss Your attempts to touch us with Your power and might. Your Word is a light unto my feet and a lamp unto my path. May I always rush to Your Word for guidance for it is food for the soul. Lord, I pray to be like a child and seek the kingdom of heaven and its righteousness with a pure heart. Speak to me, O Lord, and guide me in Your Holy Spirit. In Christ's name.

Amen.

—REVEREND CHESTINA MITCHELL ARCHIBALD

The writing of this prayer was inspired by John 1:4: "In him was life; and the life was the light of humankind." Reverend Archibald recalls how Jesus attempted to show the people of His time that there was no point in studying the Scriptures if they did not carry over what they had learned into everyday life; if you become too involved in facts and laws, you may miss a miracle happening right in front of you.

LEAD ME TO CALVARY

King of my life I crown Thee now—
Thine shall the glory be;
Lest I forget thy thorn-crowned brow,
Lead me to Calvary,
Show me the tomb where Thou wast laid,
Tenderly mourned and wept;
Angels in robes of light arrayed
Guarded Thee whilst Thou slept.
Let me, like Mary, through the gloom,
Come with a gift to Thee;
Show to me now the empty tomb—
Lead me to Calvary.
May I be willing, Lord, to bear
Daily my cross for Thee;
Even Thy cup of grief to share—
Thou hast borne all for me.
Lest I forget Gethsemane,
Lest I forget Thine agony,
Lest I forget Thy love for me,
lead me to Calvary.

—JENNIE EVELYN HUSSEY (1874–?)

Born in Henniker, New Hampshire, Jennie Evelyn Hussey was a poet and writer whose work was featured in publications such as *The Writer, Pittsburgh Christian Advocate, Zion's Herald,* and *American Forests and Forest Life.* She also contributed her writing to numerous collections of hymns.

JUST A CLOSER WALK WITH THEE

Just a closer walk with Thee;
Grant it, Jesus, if you please,
Daily walking close with Thee,
Let it be, dear Lord, let it be.
I am weak but Thou art strong,
Jesus, keep me from all wrong,
I'll be satisfied as long,
As I walk, Let me walk close with Thee.
Through this world of toils and snares,
If I falter, Lord, who cares?
Who with me my burdens shares?
None but Thee, dear Lord, none but Thee.
When my feeble life is o'er,
Time for me won't be no more,
Guide me gently, safely o'er,
To Thy kingdom shore, to Thy shore.

—TRADITIONAL SONG

This spiritual illustrates the way in which God is always with us, guiding us along our way and protecting us with His love from any harm we may encounter.

A Prayer

O Thou who art most Holy and most High!
"Let the words of our mouth and the supplication of our
    hearts—
be acceptable in Thy sight—
O Lord, our strength and Redeemer."

—Caesar Clark

Born in Louisiana, Caesar Clark has been a pastor at the Good Street Baptist Church in Dallas, Texas, for more than forty-seven years. In addition, he has been general chairman of the Baptist Ministers' Union's annual citywide revival for the past thirty years.

A Prayer for the Soul

Almighty and Merciful Father,
One whose infinite power
And wisdom transcends from
Eternity to eternity,
We come as a wayward traveler,
Seeking refuge in your Everlasting arms of
mercy and grace.
We ask that
You would penetrate our sin-sick
Souls, examine them, and heal them.
Give us good intentions, pure and
Noble, for the good of humanity.
Thank you, dear Father,
We know that you can and
We know that you will.

—Reverend Lillie Kate Benitez

Reverend Benitez's work has been featured in an anthology of the twenty-one best black poets of the twentieth century, *Understanding the New Black Poetry*. In 1981, she was the recipient of the Governor's Award in the Arts for the state of Georgia.

LORD, FREE ME FROM HARMFUL HABITS

Lord, often we begin to think of something, then we say it, then we act on it. Sometimes, we act on it over and over until it becomes a habit. Lord, teach us to keep our minds stayed on Thee and the good of Your creation; that our thoughts may be noble and our words uplifting and our deeds be those of service to others. May our acts which become habits lead us to the true sainthood and servanthood pleasing in Thy sight. Lord, my people sometimes have the habit of cursing themselves with their mouths. Lord, if they have nothing good or positive to say, please teach them to hush. In Jesus' name I pray.

　　Amen.

—REVEREND CHESTINA MITCHELL ARCHIBALD

Rash actions performed without thinking can often become habit, but we must look to God for guidance in forming holy habits in place of undesirable ones. As demonstrated in Isaiah 28:26: "God doth instruct . . . to discretion, and doth teach . . ."

A PRAYER AGAINST PROCRASTINATION

My Savior, I surrender myself anew. Teach me to utilize my time that I might be saved from procrastination. Give entrenchment to my thoughts and temperance to my words. Let my actions become diligently faithful that I may execute all matters in both an orderly and timely manner until your divine purpose for my life is complete and fulfilled. Take my desired taste for procrastination and fill me with renewed passion and love for you.

William Williams expressed my deepest desire when he wrote, "Guide me, O Thou great Jehovah, pilgrim through this barren land. I am weak, but Thou art mighty; hold me with Thy powerful hand."

—REVEREND DR. ROLAND LONG

A native of Mississippi, Reverend Long is presently pastor at Clarke Memorial United Methodist Church in Nashville, Tennessee. In his ministry, he is primarily interested in evangelism, with a focus on spiritual empowerment.

PRAYER TO END PROCRASTINATION

Almighty and Merciful God,
We confess that we have done little with the talents and gifts that Thou hath so graciously bestowed upon us. We have not made the best of the time You have so graciously given us. We have procrastinated to the point that even our best intentions have gone awry. Lord, help our unbelief—strengthen our faith. We know now that lack of productivity is often equated to lack of faith. Lord, lend again Your creative hand as we become Your instruments of healing and beauty working diligently to make Your world a better place for all.

Grant us now Your spirit of earnest discipline as we set aside all that would keep us from being the best we can be and making the most of what You have given us. In Thy Holy Name we pray.
 Amen.

—REVEREND CHESTINA MITCHELL ARCHIBALD

Inspiration for this prayer was found in Proverbs 6:10–11: "Yet a little sleep, a little slumber, a little folding of the hands to sleep: so shall thy poverty come as one that travelleth, and thy want as an armed man." A strong faith in God leads to a productive use of the gifts and talents He has given each and every one of us.

AGAINST THE CURSE OF DRUNKENNESS

Defend, O Lord, this Thy land from the curse of drunkenness. Guide aright the oft misguided enthusiasm of those, beneath whose striving lies the terrible truth of our national weakness. Let the life of him who was born one hundred years ago this night live as both warning and inspiration to the young—the beauty of his song, the wonder of his genius, the shame of his slavery to drink. We are glad of his life even though he sinned, but we tremble at the strength of his and our weakness, O God, and pray for Thy strength.

Amen.

—W. E. B. Du Bois (1868–1963)

Among the highlights of his career, W. E. B. Du Bois served as director of publications and editor of *Crisis* magazine, which the NAACP used to voice its demands for educational, political, and social reform. He also demonstrated his civil rights activism by participating in marches in protest of injustice against blacks. The person he refers to in his prayer is Edgar Allan Poe, born January 18, 1809.

Fix Our Hearts

O Lord of lords, King of kings, to You we pray. We pray that Your Sovereignty will be made known to all of humanity. It is our desire to see that Your kingdom reigns here on earth. We know that without You there can be no joy, no peace, and no harmony; but with You, we can be the people of God and live in a kingdom not made by human hands. O Lord, fix our hearts so that Your spirit may dwell within us and Your kingdom be made known to all people. In the name of Jesus, Who commanded not His will, but Your will be done, we also pray, Lord, that it is not our will, but Yours that is done. In and through Christ we pray.

Amen.

—Reverend Chestina Mitchell Archibald

This quote from Matthew 26:39 illustrates the theme of this prayer: "O my Father, if it be possible, let this cup pass from me: nevertheless not as I will, but as thou wilt." An unyielding love for God creates the fervent desire to see His will be done on earth.

Prayer to Be Free of Drugs, Gambling, or Any Addiction

Come by here, Lord, someone needs you. Permeate our minds with thy Holy Spirit that we may learn to depend only upon thee. Lord, we know that through you all things are possible—wash away these desires and impure spirits that attack our mental, physical, and spiritual being. Teach us to be dependent upon nothing but thee. Anoint us anew, let thy spirit fall afresh on us that we may rise in mind, body, and spirit being as pure as gold—free from addictions. Thank you, dear God, for deliverance one day at a time. In the precious name of Jesus, we pray.

Amen.

—Reverend Kennard Murray

Reverend Murray is a mental health specialist for the state of Tennessee. He is licensed in the areas of both psychology and religion and integrates these two subjects in his work with mentally ill patients.

A Prayer for the Strength to Abstain

Lord, why is there such a thing as alcohol? It is so destructive. Many begin to consume this fire in small portions, and gradually escalate in this consumption until they are consumed in mind, body, and spirit. Homes and communities are destroyed by it. None is made better. Lord, take away the desire for this poison which is so destructive. Lord, I intercede for others and come now repenting of this destructive habit, and looking to You for complete deliverance of body, soul, and spirit. Break the generational curse of alcohol abuse. Fulfill these empty souls, so that they will not seek after You in artificial, unfulfilling ways. Reveal Your will and purpose for their lives, so that they may live a life that is useful and pleasing to You. Truly, fill the void in these lives with Your Spirit. Help them to recognize the reality of Your love and the falseness of alcohol's seduction. Lord, transform these lives and empower them to live according to Your will, in Jesus' name.

Amen.

—Reverend Chestina Mitchell Archibald

This prayer deals with the subject of alcohol abuse, an unfortunately common problem in today's society. When we are tempted to overindulge in alcohol, it is helpful to keep Ephesians 5:18 in mind: "And be not drunk with wine, wherein is excess; but be filled with the Spirit."

TEMPTATION AND THE SPIRIT

Lord, the body is weak. I do not want to sin against Thee. Continue, O Lord, to strengthen my mind, body, and spirit so that I remain chaste before Thee. I submit my body and my desires to the subjection of the Spirit. Lord, I know with every temptation You provide a way of escape, and I know that there is no temptation which can overtake me. May both my words and my deeds glorify Thee and may nothing take precedence over fulfilling Your will for my life. In the love and mighty name of Jesus, I pray.

Amen.

—Reverend Chestina Mitchell Archibald

Reverend Archibald reflected on James 1:12 when writing this prayer: "Blessed is the [person] that endureth temptation: for when he is tired, he shall receive the crown of life, which the Lord hath promised to them that love him." The rewards that we would receive if we gave into temptation are nothing compared to God's reward for honoring Him and remaining steadfast in faith.

ADULTERY

My God, My God, Your weak servant comes before Thee acknowledging that I have yielded to my flesh. I have looked upon another's body and savored its warmth. I have touched another's hand, and caressed another intimately, and at that same time have neglected to be mindful of the attention needed by my own spouse. Forgive me, Lord. Turn my affections back to the mate of my youth. In Jesus' name I pray.

Amen.

—REVEREND CHESTINA MITCHELL ARCHIBALD

The theme of this prayer is the sinfulness of adultery and the need to seek forgiveness from God for breaking His commandment. The prayer was influenced by God's commandment in Exodus 20:14: "Thou shalt not commit adultery."

A Prayer Against Anger

Praise God, Hallelujah, thanks for your mighty deed, we glorify, we magnify thy name. We come to thee asking thy blessing on us. Forgive all who are angry with their brothers and sisters with or without cause. May we have forgiveness and strength to ask for our brothers' and sisters' forgiveness. Let us never forget how much thou hast forgiven us. Lord, look down on us in love and peace. Please bless my brothers and sisters and cause us to reconcile in peace and love in the precious name of Jesus.

Amen.

—Reverend Vattina Parker and Cheryl Wylie

Reverend Vattina Parker is a minister at Greater Rock Creek Baptist Church in Mount Rainier, Maryland. Cheryl Wylie is a minister at Spirit of Faith Christian Center in Washington, D.C. This prayer recognizes the importance of finding forgiveness in ourselves before expecting to inspire it in others. It also recognizes that God himself sets the example and provides inspiration to offer true forgiveness.

A PRAYER FOR SELF-RESTRAINT

I come to You in repentance, dear Lord. I completely lost my temper with my beautiful children today. It was not their fault, yet I yelled at them and intimidated them in a fit of uncontrolled anger. Help them to forgive me and know my love for them, even if I sometimes lose my temper. Please help me to control my anger. I know no one deserves to be mistreated. I do not want to act rashly based on negative emotions. I beg for Your intervention when anger begins to rise in my heart. Let me reflect on my anger before it escapes and let me realize its futility and the damage it causes others. I pray this sincerely and humbly in Christ's Name.

Amen.

—REVEREND CHESTINA MITCHELL ARCHIBALD

At times we all lose control of our baser emotions, but we must be mindful of God's will and attempt to think before we act. Speaking rashly in anger is a negative way to deal with unpleasant emotions, as Proverbs 18:7 clearly reminds us: "A fool's mouth is his destruction, and his lips are the snare of his soul."

FOLLOWING GOD'S WILL

1. Shall I for fear of feeble man,
The spirit's course in me restrain?
Or, undismay'd in deed and word,
Be a true witness of my Lord.

2. Aw'd by mortal's frown, shall I
Conceal the word of God Most High!
How then before thee shall I dare
To stand, or how thy anger bear?

3. Shall I, to soothe th' unholy throng,
Soften the truth, or smooth my tongue,
To gain earth's gilded toys or, flee
The cross endur'd, my Lord, by thee?

4. What then is he whose scorn I dread?
Whose wrath or hate makes me afraid
A man! an heir of death! a slave
To sin! A bubble on the wave!

5. Yea, let men rage, since thou will spread
Thy shadowing wings around my head:
Since in all pain thy tender love
Will still my sure refreshment prove.

—DAVID WALKER (1785–1830)

David Walker was born free in North Carolina and later settled in Boston. His *Appeal*, an antislavery pamphlet that called on slaves to revolt against their oppressors, is considered one of the most powerful documents in early American history.

MY PRAYER

Father, we thank Thee that Thou are our Father.
We commit ourselves to Thee.
May Thy spirit of absolute purity, absolute honesty,
absolute unselfishness, absolute love permeate our lives.
May we join our hands and our hearts with the peoples of the world
to build a fellowship of freedom, of peace, of love, of brotherhood
    everywhere.
    Amen.

—MARY MCLEOD BETHUNE (1875–1955)

Among other notable points of her career, Mary McLeod Bethune was appointed the director of Negro Affairs Division of the National Youth Administration by Franklin D. Roosevelt during his first term as president. She later served in the Roosevelt administration in several other key positions, and was always a welcome visitor at the White House.

LORD, YOU ARE THE HIGHEST AUTHORITY

Lord, when I seek to rule over myself, may I always be mindful that You are the ultimate authority and all must bow to Thee. Therefore, I fret not about what humans seek to do to me, for all must be accountable to Thee.

There are places that humans call high. There are persons whom humans call "boss." Lord, thanks for giving me the consciousness that no place is high unless You are there and no person shall reign over me. I work because I work for Thee, I obey because I am obeying Thee. You are my only authority and to You only do I surrender all.

Lord, teach me to respect all Your creatures and extend to them love that You have placed within me. Help me to recognize the rules and regulations of society in order that my conduct may not be disruptive when justice is being done. Yet, let me reject unfairness and be willing to work to rectify the situation.

   Amen.

—REVEREND CHESTINA MITCHELL ARCHIBALD

Reverend Archibald found the motivation for writing this prayer in Psalms 27:1: "The Lord is my light and my salvation; whom shall I fear? The Lord is the strength of my life; of whom shall I be afraid?" We are reminded that regardless of our varying degrees of authority here on earth, there is only one true "boss."

HELP ME SHARE IN YOUR VICTORY, O LORD

Lord, thank You for the victory of Christ over death. Through this resurrection, righteousness prevailed over evil and thus all are given hope. Grant us victory of love over hate, faith over fear, truth over lies, and strength over weakness. O God, as You led the Israelites to victory in war, please lead us to Your promised land. The war we fight is without blades. Your truth is our sword. May our lives be consecrated to help bring victory over evil. Bless our efforts, we pray. In Christ's Name.

Amen.

—REVEREND CHESTINA MITCHELL ARCHIBALD

Inspiration for writing this prayer came from Psalms 28:7: "The Lord is my strength and my shield; my heart trusted in Him, and I am helped: therefore my heart greatly rejoiceth; and with my song will I praise Him." With God's help, His followers continue to fight daily for the triumph of good over evil.

GOD'S ROLE IN OUR LIVES

When I seek abundance in my life, I must be linked with the source of all good. When I am separated from the Source, I cannot bear fruit. That which is separated withers and dies. To bear fruit, I must abide in the Christ consciousness and feed on the Word. When I do this, whatever I ask, I will receive.

I must emulate the Christ. I must give up everything that is unlike the Christ. I must forgive myself and others. I must be patient. I must be kind. I must be loving. I must be peaceful. A kind word turneth away wrath. I must look beyond appearances and behold the good. I have faith in Christ who lives in me. I abide in the Christ and experience peace and freedom. Thank you, Father.

—REVEREND CARMEN YOUNG

This prayer is an excerpt from "Divine Thoughts," a small collection of daily inspirational prayers written by Reverend Young. She offers John 15:5 as her source of motivation in writing this prayer: "I am the vine, ye are the branches: He that abideth in me, and I in him, the same bringeth much fruit."

LORD, HELP ME OVERCOME

Lord, God Almighty,

There is a wrestling match within my soul. You are fighting and Satan is fighting and I am somewhere in the middle fighting you both. Wrestling with a visible foe is far easier than with one who cannot be seen. Satan is even willing to let people believe he does not exist as long as they are caught in his web. Lord, I pray to stop fighting You and to wholeheartedly join forces with You to kick Satan's influence out of my soul. Lord, I love You. Yet, Satan sneaks in and gets his hold. Please protect me from his attacks. Only You have the power to win over his evil, so I ask You to drive him out and strengthen my soul to resist him. In Christ's Name.

    Amen.

—REVEREND CHESTINA MITCHELL ARCHIBALD

James 4:7 sums up the theme of this prayer: "Resist the devil, and he will flee from you." The evils in today's society tempt people to commit sinful acts, but with God's help, we can resist Satan's lure.

You Must Be Pure and Holy

1. When I was wicked and prone to sin,
My Lord, brethren, Ah, my Lord.
I thought that I couldn't be born again,
My Lord, brethren, Ah, my Lord.
You must be pure and holy, you must be pure and holy,
You must be pure and holy to see God feed his lambs.

2. I'll run all round the cross and cry
My Lord, brethren, Ah, my Lord.
O give me some peace before I die,
My Lord, brethren, Ah, my Lord.
You must be pure and holy, you must be pure and holy,
You must be pure and holy to see God feed his lambs.

3. The Devil am I liar and conjurer, too,
My Lord, brethren, Ah, my Lord.
If you don't look out, he'll conjure you through,
My Lord, brethren, Ah, my Lord.
You must be pure and holy, you must be pure and holy,
You must be pure and holy to see God feed his lambs.

4. O run up, sonny, and get your crown
My Lord, brethren, Ah, my Lord.
And by your Father sit you down.
My Lord, brethren, Ah, my Lord.
You must be pure and holy, you must be pure and holy,
You must be pure and holy to see God feed his lambs.

5. I was pretty young when I began,
My Lord, brethren, Ah, my Lord.

But now my work is almost done.
My Lord, brethren, Ah, my Lord.
You must be pure and holy, you must be pure and holy,
You must be pure and holy to see God feed his lambs.

6. The Devil's mad and I am glad,
My Lord, brethren, Ah, my Lord.
He lost his soul he thought he had.
My Lord, brethren, Ah, my Lord.
You must be pure and holy, you must be pure and holy,
You must be pure and holy to see God feed his lambs.

7. Go 'way, Satan, I don't mind you,
My Lord, brethren, Ah, my Lord.
You wonder, too, that you can't go through.
My Lord, brethren, Ah, my Lord.
You must be pure and holy, you must be pure and holy,
You must be pure and holy to see God feed his lambs.

8. A lily-white stone came rolling down,
My Lord, brethren, Ah, my Lord.
It rolled like thunder through the town.
My Lord, brethren, Ah, my Lord.
You must be pure and holy, you must be pure and holy,
You must be pure and holy to see God feed his lambs.

—TRADITIONAL SPIRITUAL

This prayer demonstrates that, although we may fall into sin, God will always give us the strength to turn our backs on evil and to turn our gaze toward Him for guidance. Thus, we may become pure and holy in His eyes and one day enter into His kingdom.

OF THANKS AND PRAISE

THANKS AND PRAISE TO YOU, O GOD

Lord God of Heaven
We Praise and thank You for all great and simple joys
For the gift of wonder and the joy of discovery
For every fresh experience
for all that comes to us through sympathy and through sorrow
And for the joy of work and achievement.
For music, poems, church workers, friends and foes
And for all who work in one form or another to increase the beauty
of life.

For the likeness of Christ in ordinary people, for their forbearance,
courage and kindness
And for all humble and obscure lives of service.
We give You all the glory, praise and honor,
In the name of Jesus,
Amen.

—REVEREND CHESTINA MITCHELL ARCHIBALD

The writing of this prayer was inspired by Psalms 100:4–5: "Enter into his gates
with thanksgiving, and into his courts with praise: be thankful unto him, and
bless his name. For the Lord is good; his mercy is everlasting; and his truth
endureth to all generations."

PRAYER OF THANKSGIVING

God of Love who reaches out to your straying children; God of Grace who forgives and saves us; God of Light who shattered the darkness about us, accept our worship and prayers before thee as we come with bowed heads and humble hearts and lives open to your still small voice which gives us eternal life.

We come, O God, before your throne of grace, thanking you for those moments, expected and unplanned, when your light shone brightly and our foggy minds became clear, and you made so much that we desired possible. We thank you for your grace when moments of friendship were created and bonded, projects were planned, implemented and finalized, dreams found fruition, hopes took shape, beliefs were affirmed, risks brought reward, love and peace became a reality!

O we bless your Holy Name for those surprises of delight that enriched our days and nights. May we never stop praising and thanking you for the unexpected blessings you give to us.

Now, Lord, when we failed to thank you for all things, please forgive us and let your Spirit convict us. Give us strength, grace, wisdom and love to affirm our relationship with you and each other by prayer, kind deeds, unselfish acts and service through love. Bless us, we pray, with prosperity and obedience to your will so that others may know your love through our witness. In Jesus' name we pray. Amen.

—REVEREND DR. ROSA B. CLEMENTS

Reverend Clements is currently serving as pastor of North Hill United Methodist Church in Akron, Ohio. She is a member of many organizations, including the International Society of Theta Chi, NAACP, Black Methodists for Church Renewal, and Black Pastors' Fellowship.

A Prayer of Thankfulness

Almighty and Everlasting God,
How can I begin to thank You for Your abundant blessings? Ne'er could I repay the gift of life! The Blessings which flow freely from You are numerous. You are such a generous God. Thanks for the abundant love and blessings You give. Lord, I offer my heartfelt thanks for Your gifts, both physical and spiritual. Thank You for awakening my heart and spirit to the awareness of Your presence. Lord, because of You life has meaning, and is filled with hope, formed with purpose, and brimming with potential. In gratitude, I offer my life anew. In Christ's Name.

    Amen.

—Reverend Chestina Mitchell Archibald

In writing this prayer, Reverend Archibald reflected on Psalms 118:1: "O give thanks unto the Lord; for [God] is good: because [God's] mercy endureth for ever." The prayer reminds us of the many gifts He has given us, and how we must thank Him each day by trying to please Him with our actions.

PRAYER OF PRAISE AND THANKSGIVING

O Lord, I praise You today for Your goodness!
You are great and greatly to be praised!
I love You, I honor You, and I worship You.
For You alone are the Living God.
There is none beside You.
You are God and I bless You, my Lord,
Awesome Trinity, Holy Mystery,
God the Father, God the Son, and God the Holy Spirit.
This is the day You have made, I will rejoice and be glad in it.
Father, I thank You for loving me, and giving me the gift of life.
Lord Jesus, I thank You for Your wonderful gift of salvation.
Holy Spirit, I thank You for Your powerful Presence.
My heart is overwhelmed with love for You, my God.
I pause in the busyness of life just to thank You,
To praise You, and to worship You!
Let everything within me bless Your holy Name!
My words can not express all I want to say, but I will say
I love You, Lord,
For You are good and Your mercy toward me is great!
I give you all the glory, the honor, and the praise!
In the Name of Jesus I pray,
    Amen.

—BISHOP CHARLES E. BLAKE

When Bishop Blake first became pastor of the West Angeles Church of God in Christ in Los Angeles, California, in 1969, he had a congregation of fifty; today the church boasts more than fifteen thousand members, making it the largest Church of God in Christ in the world. In 1985, he began serving as bishop of the First Jurisdiction of Southern California, overseeing almost 270 churches. In addition to his numerous involvements in the community, he has also been the recipient of many honors, including being listed by *Ebony* magazine as one of America's 15 Greatest Black Preachers in 1984, and in 1996 he was noted as one of the most powerful black men in Los Angeles by *L.A. Focus Magazine*.

A TRADITIONAL PRAYER

Today! Our Heavenly Father, it is once more and again a few of your hand-made servants are gathered in this sacred place, knee bent and body bowed, in the humblest manner that we know how. Our heads hung from the locks of our shoulder facing mother dust and avoiding greedy-grave once more in this life. We thank you for this day; a day that we have never seen before, but one that has been coming since the dawn of creation.

We thank thee, master, that all night long angels of mercy watched over us while we slumbered and slept. We thank you for keeping us from all harm, hurt, and danger. Early this morning, you touched us with your finger of Divine love and we awoke to discover that the blood was still running warm in our veins.

We thank thee, master, that our beds were not our cooling-boards and our bed-clothes were not our winding sheets, and the four walls of our bedrooms were not the narrow confines of the greedy-grave.

My master! It was you who lengthened our prickly threads of our lives and bid our golden moments to roll on a little longer for Jesus' sake.

Now, Jesus! Now, Jesus! If you see anything like sin lurking anywhere near us, drive it as far from us as east is from west, and throw it into the sea of forgetfulness, where it will never rise to face us in the present world, or condemn us as the judgement bar.

Build us up where we are torn down; strengthen us where we are weak; prop us up on the ever leaning side of Jesus.

Bless our pastor; turpentine his head with oil of understanding. Set him on a hallowed fire. Let him down in your rich store-house where he can bring treasures, both old and new for the edifying of our people.

Let him declare your truth between the living and the dead. Bear him up on eagle's wing. Let him fly in spirit, between Sun, Moon, and Stars. Let Heaven and Earth come together in this place right now.

And now, Lord, when you've cared for the sick, the lowly in spirit; when you've done going and coming, caring, and loving for the whole wide universal world, remember my children and my faithful companion. Lord, then, remember this your humble servant; who is the least of all. I am weak, but you are strong; and my feeble, weak, and sinful condition is ever before me.

And now, Lord, when it's time to go into my dying room, never to come out no more. When I am through making tracks in this sandy land. When our feeble voices and our dried tongues are cleaved and tightened to the roofs of our mouths; when the battles of this life have been fought and won, meet me down at the river, where there ain't no bridge. Tell Jordan to behave herself. And then, master, we'll get on board the Old Ship of Zion and go reeling and rocking into the kingdom of heaven.

And then Master—Somewhere—where the universe has an epileptic spasm.
Somewhere—where the moon melts and runs down like blood.
Somewhere—where time shall be no more
Meet us, master, in the land where we'll never grow old.
Meet us in the land where the wicked shall cease from troubling
And the weary shall be at rest.
Somewhere—where every day will be Sunday, and no bossman to call Monday.
Somewhere—where the Sabbath will not end.
Meet us in that land where we'll never grow old.

Meet us in that land where we will sit at the feet of angels and
We'll look on the sweet face of Jesus.

Somewhere—where we will bathe our sweet souls in the sea of
    Heavenly rest.
This is your Servant's Prayer, master.
So I hope, So it be.
Amen and Thank God.

This prayer was found among the papers of an old Baptist deacon after his death
in 1880. The prayer gives thanks and praise to God for all of the love He has
bestowed upon us, and demonstrates the divine power of faith.

DEDICATION

God,
you have given us
very life and salvation!
All we have to respond with
is inadequate

                              for your great gifts

Although we can not repay you
we still want to respond
to the extent we can
pass your Spirit along . . .

And though even in this
we must ask your assistance—
take us and use us
to do your bidding!

We have sought to pray
in the Spirit of Jesus,
    Amen.

—REVEREND WILL E. CHAMBERS

The third section of *Prayer Portions*, this prayer offers dedication of our lives to God in order to repay Him and show our appreciation for all He has given us. Reverend Chambers's poetry has been featured in anthologies including *Treasury of Poetry, East of Sunrise, Tracing Shadows,* and *Meditations,* and he has also authored several books.

A PRAYER OF THE ORDINARY

Dear God, to whom I owe all allegiance and praise. To whom all glory and honor and majesty belong. I yet love your tender appearing. Thou who created the great and the small. The only God who creates something from seemingly nothingness and nobodiness. Thou art great and wonderful.

To experience you in all of your glory and power, I must take time to recognize and to thank you for being involved in the mundane and simple things in my life. I must thank you. For I heard you speak in the simple ordinary sound of a drill as it tore up the concrete outside my window. I heard you say that as a worker tears up the cement in order to rebuild anew, that sometimes in my life you must tear down in order to rebuild me in your image. For this I am thankful and appreciative. I thank you for entering into my slumbered breathing as I wait on my knees to hear from you. I thank you simply for the food that strengthens my body, the wonderful books that feed my mind, the fellowship with you that feeds my spirit, the love of a mate that enchants my living, the sound of music that graces my ears, the smile of the wind that brushes my being, the gentleness of your sunshine that causes me to sigh, the dying of my body and yet the evolution of my mind. For these ordinary events I thank you. I now confess as Job once confessed, that once I heard of thee, but now my eyes have seen thee. In the name of Jesus, keep me aware of the ordinary.

Amen.

—REVEREND H. CARLYLE CHURCH, JR.

In addition to his other awards and achievements, Reverend Church was the winner of The National Anthology of Poetry Contest in both 1995 and 1996. He is also the author of a book, *In The Black*.

THANK YOU . . .

Dear God, thank You for all the blessings You have bestowed upon me.

I thank You for the strength, creativity, insight, and wisdom You have given me and ask that You continue to watch over and guide me.

I thank You for the courage to move on even when I'm not sure where I'm headed.

I thank You for the understanding that without the bad, I'd never fully appreciate the good (and thank You for teaching me to finally enjoy the good).

Thank You for the loved ones in my life (especially my mother and father), for I now recognize them as my guardian angels.

As Your Spirit works through me, I promise to continue to spread Your positive energy and love with an open heart to friends, strangers, loved ones, and adversaries.

To whom much is given much is expected, and I am eternally grateful for Your gifts.

Peace, Love, and Blessings. Amen.

—MALCOLM-JAMAL WARNER

Best known for his role as Theo in one of America's most popular television sitcoms, *The Cosby Show*, Malcolm-Jamal Warner currently stars in his own show, *Malcolm and Eddie*. In addition to television and film acting, he also has spent time on the other side of the camera, directing episodes of *The Cosby Show*, *Sesame Street*, *The Fresh Prince of Bel-Air*, and Nickelodeon's *All That*. He also directed Arsenio Hall and Magic Johnson in an AIDS awareness video, *Timeout: The Truth About HIV, AIDS, and You*. He was presented the Key of Life Award at the twenty-fifth Annual NAACP Image Awards, as a tribute to his work.

THANKSGIVING

Wellspring of everything,
our blessings
come every day,
some unnoticed until taken away,
and others in disguise
as struggles and hardship
that make us wise.

When we begin naming them the
list is endless
we often end up saying, as now—
Father, you know what they are.

Words are inadequate
but since you see us
inside and out
you know what this is all about—
a feeble effort to say "thank you"
from a sincere heart.

—Reverend Will E. Chambers

This prayer is the fourth section of Reverend Chambers's work *Prayer Portions,* which is "written in free verse and serves as a prayer primer." He has been pastor at several churches and has taught religion courses at Livingstone and Miles Colleges.

AFFECTION

Our Father, which art in heaven, we thank you for your constant care and watchfulness. We thank you, Lord God, for your word which declares, "You will teach us and instruct us in the way thou shalt go and your eyes will guide us." This constant care only comes because of your concern for us, and you want the best for us. Father, we thank you for being able to stand under the shadow of the Most High God. For then we can truly say "you are our shield and buckler." Protect us from ourselves as much as others. Keep us in the center of thy holy will, and encamp your angels around and about us. You are Jehovah Shammah, the one who will never leave us or forsake us. For this promise of affection we are truly thankful.

Amen.

—MINISTER ANTHONY GREEN

As the chaplain for a correctional institution in Vicksburg, Mississippi, Anthony Green concentrates his ministry on young people, helping them to know God and teaching them how to love Him. The reference in his prayer to Jehovah Shammah (which means "The Lord Is There") comes from the last verse in Ezekiel. Jehovah Shammah is another name for God, specifically referring to His relational nature or what He wants to be for His people.

TO THE ONE

U who made the worlds and all that is in
them
i thank U for the life/power beauty that
manifest this body and sustains it
i thank U for the joy of living
i thank you for the job of being
i thank U for the harmony/power that
is my
thought and action
thank U for the love that is the life
and health/prosperity of all my beloveds
thanks
for the wealth that delights and clears my material
obligations
thanks for the faith that shines
in my life and makes life an adventure
with U
thanks that U bless my friends and
teach the enemy to leave
us be
thanks because my dedication to law
is vindicated
b-4 the scoffers
thanks for the blessings beyond description
& prescriptions
for which i may have asked
thank you that I am that
that pleases U

& for the consciousness
of Your presence thank U whose love
i am

—DELBERT TIBBS

Delbert Tibbs has been active in the human rights movement, as well as being a
tireless abolitionist against the death penalty. A friend describes him as a "religious mystic"; Tibbs describes himself as a "sinner who loves the Great Spirit."

ABUNDANCE

Lord, You have blessed me with every spiritual blessing and with an abundance for every good work. You have so generously given me the opportunity to live the abundant life through You. I pray that I may be a blessing to others and share the abundance that You have given me. Help me, Lord, to see the needs of others and meet them when it is wise to do so.

Amen.

—REVEREND CHESTINA MITCHELL ARCHIBALD

Reverend Archibald cites John 10:10b as giving her encouragement in writing this prayer: "I am come that they might have life, and that they might have it more abundantly." The best way to show our appreciation for all that God has given us is to share our gifts with others.

CARETAKER FOR THE NIGHT

O God, thank you for having brought me through the night. You were there. (Breathe) No other help could be found. No other help could have come. No other help could have stayed present to the
> crying
> releasing
> cleansing of my soul.

(Breathe, breathe)
Thank you for not abandoning me. Now into this new day, take me through second by second.
> Amen. (Breathe)

—REVEREND JULIA A. PRINCE

Reverend Prince, of George W. Long Memorial Presbyterian Church in Cheraw, South Carolina, explains the theme of her prayer: "This prayer affirms for me that family, friends, and others may care and want to be there. Yet, there are moments when only the divine Helper can and will come."

On Aging

Thank You, thank You, thank You, Lord. For I have witnessed many rising and settings of the sun. I have seen changes take place not only in this my body, but in the world in which I live. Of all these changes, I thank You most for the changes that have taken place in my soul. I, like Your servant of old, have learned to be abased and abound in whatever state I find myself there to be content.

I thank You for memories of those that have gone before and pray Your blessing on my offsprings yet unborn.

Lord, You have kept me here for a reason. Make clear Your will. I have no reason for being except to serve Thee and that I do with much joy.

Amen.

—Reverend Chestina Mitchell Archibald

We are wise to honor the aged; by learning to respect them, we are preparing ourselves to experience respect as we age. "Honour thy father and thy mother: that thy days may be long upon the land which the Lord thy God giveth thee" (Exodus 20:12).

A HEART THAT PRAISES GOD

O God of Grace and God of Mercy,

We humbly bow before you
to give you thanks and praises.

We give thanks
for the countless blessings
and the numerous gifts you have bestowed upon us.

We give thanks
In our times of Joy, and in our times of Sadness;
In our times of Victory, and in our times of Defeat;
In our times of Success, and in our times of Failure;
In our times of Pain; and in our times of Sorrow.

We give thanks for eyes to see your beautiful creations;
To see the birds as they grace the heavens, and the fish
as they navigate through the seas' highways,
To see the flowers burst into bloom and the trees spring
forth with new life.

We give thanks
for arms to reach, hands to touch and hold,
for legs to walk and ears to hear.

We give thanks
Thanks, when we are glad and thanks when we are sad.
Thanks when our purse is full and thanks when our purse is empty.
Thanks when we are in good health and thanks when illness
    overcomes us.

We give thanks and praise in our winning and in our losing
for being first and for being last.

We give thanks for the gift of friendship;
when they stand by us and when they walk away.
Lord, we give thanks.

Thanks for all the gifts that flow so freely
both day and night in our lives.

Lord today, we give thanks with our whole heart!
Thanks, because we are refilled with gratitude for the things you
have sent to us, for the hope we feel in hopeless situations; for
watching over us and protecting us day and night.

We give thanks for you provisions of food, shelter, and
clothing, for your comforting presence and Your divine love.

We give thanks and praise in the name of your dear Son Jesus
Who died and overcame the cross that we may have life and
have life more abundantly! We give thanks.
    Amen.

—REVEREND DR. DAN STEVENSON

Reverend Stevenson, of Savannah, Georgia, explains his inspiration in the writing
of this prayer: "When I think of how good the Lord has been to me, I can only
write a prayer of praise and thanksgiving; a prayer giving God thanks for all His
many blessings."

ACTS OF LOVE

O Infinite amiableness! When shall I love Thee without bounds? Without coldness or interruption, which, alas! So often seize me here below? Let me never suffer any creature to be Thy rival, or to share my heart with Thee; let me have no other God, no other love, but only Thee.

Whoever loves, desires to please the beloved object; and according to the degree of love is the greatness of desire; make me, O God! diligent and earnest in pleasing Thee; let me cheerfully discharge the most painful and costly duties; and forsake friends, riches, ease and life itself, rather than disobey Thee.

Whoever loves, desires the welfare and happiness of the beloved object; but Thou, O dear Jesus, canst receive no addition from my imperfect services; what shall I do to express my affection towards Thee? I will relieve the necessities of my poor brethren, who are members of Thy body; for he that loveth not his brother who he has seen, how can he love God whom he hath not seen?

O, Crucified Jesus! In whom I live, and without whom I die: mortify in me all sensual desires; inflame my heart with Thy holy love, that I may no longer esteem the vanities of this world, but place my affections entirely on Thee.

Let my last breath, when my soul shall leave my body, breathe forth love to Thee, my God; I entered into life without acknowledging Thee, let me therefore finish it in loving Thee; O let the last act of life be love, remembering that God is love.

—RIGHT REVEREND RICHARD ALLEN (1760–1831)

Born a slave to a Quaker lawyer, Richard Allen went on to become a licensed preacher and the first bishop of the African Methodist Episcopal Church in 1787. The lot in Philadelphia where he and other black churchgoers built the church is the oldest parcel of real estate continuously owned by African Americans in the United States.

ADORATION AND PRAISE

Our Maker,
We are ever in wonder and worship of you
because of your world
ushered in by your command
light, water, land . . . man
and even more
your initiative
through your incarnate Son
who our second chance won—
after with volition
we violated your condition . . .
Thank you for
making us yours
and reopening doors for us
We, like our hands—raise
our hearts to you in adoration and praise . . .

                 —REVEREND WILL E. CHAMBERS

This prayer, the final part of *Prayer Portions*, demonstrates praise to God for all of the wonderful gifts He has given us. Among Reverend Chambers's many honors, he was listed in *Who's Who in Religion*, was cited for creating his denomination's logo, and is a member of the Theta Phi theological honor society.

LISTEN, LORD—A PRAYER

O Lord, we come this morning
Knee-bowed and body-bent
Before thy throne of grace.
O Lord—this morning—
Bow our hearts beneath our knees,
And our knees in some lonesome valley.
We come this morning—
Like empty pitchers to a full fountain,
With no merits of our own.
O Lord—open up a new window of heaven,
And lean out far over the battlements of glory,
And listen this morning.

—JAMES WELDON JOHNSON (1871–1938)

Called the "quintessential Harlem Renaissance man," Johnson founded the first black daily paper in America, the *Daily American*, in 1895. In 1914, he became contributing editor of *New York Age*, then served as an official for the NAACP from 1916 until 1930. While with the NAACP, his notable accomplishments included fortifying the group's support in the West and South, investigating America's misrule in Haiti in 1920, and successfully lobbying for the Dyer Lynching Bill in 1922.

It's All Good

O God of Love and Power,
when we hear from your word
that everything you have made is good, it makes us feel good
about ourselves and each other.

For all of us have something to be angry about:
some of us have been abused,
and some of us have been denied justice.
Others of us have been rejected.
Our mouths have been full of angry words.
Our hearts have been colored by sin.
We had a bitter taste in our mouths.

But, then your love flooded our existence.
Your grace has provided for us.
Your mercy has unlocked doors for us.
Your forgiveness has made us a grateful people.

Thank you God. Thank you for your love.
Thank you for your mercy. You have turned our
tears into laughter, our sorrows into joy. We are healed. Thank you
    God.
All praise be unto you. In Jesus Christ's name we pray.
    Amen.

—James King

James King is director of the Conference Council Office, Tennessee Conference, the United Methodist Church. A dynamic motivational communicator, he is one of the top thinkers in this country in the area of personal and corporate leadership development. In this prayer, he comments on the way that despite the hardships that we all endure in some form, God's love can always heal us.

PRAYER FOR MORNING WORSHIP

God of Love and Dignity,

We bow before you with grateful and believing hearts. We are glad that, with all the power of the universe at your disposal, with the bounty of all that is at your magnificent hand, you yet find room in your heart for each one of us. We give you praise because your love and grace are far beyond any and all things we can imagine. We lift our heads and hearts to you this day simply because you are God. There is no other.

At times we live differently. Sometimes we behave as if there are other gods, other allegiances more important and other relationships worthy of our time and attention. We must confess that we are too often seduced and driven by the trappings of this world. We fail to give you proper glory. We fail to give you proper credence in our lives. We fall to the allure and glamour of the world, tumbling to the shame of sin. And it hurts us. It breaks me. We find that we fall far short of all that you would have us be and do.

Still, by your miraculous capacity to forgive, you call us back to your fold. God, you never give up on us and we are so grateful. You refuse to leave us. You reject notions of abandoning us. No matter what we have done, you always remind us that we are always more than the sum total of our actions before you. We thank you for this unbelievable, unimaginable yet undeniable love.

It is in this thanksgiving that we dare to ask you for our needs. Some of us need healing. Some of us need strength. Some of us need hope. So many are our needs, our desires, our dreams. But more than any of these things is our hunger to do your will, to live in your will, to be as your Son taught us to be. Strengthen us to truly seek your face, to live in your hope, to demonstrate your love. Then we can truly be called your witnesses and your people. Then we can truly be heralds of your Kingdom. This is our hope and our longing. We lift this prayer in the mighty, majestic and masterful name of Jesus the Christ.

Amen.

—REVEREND VANCE P. ROSS

Residing in Nashville, Tennessee, Reverend Ross is director of Small Group Ministries for the General Board of Discipleship for the United Methodist Church. He is also a prominent national workshop leader and conference speaker.

AN EVENING THOUGHT
Salvation by Christ, with Penitential Cries

Salvation comes by Christ alone,
The only Son of God;
Redemption now to every one,
That love his holy Word.
Dear Jesus we would fly to Thee,
And leave off every Sin,
Thy tender mercy well agree;
Salvation from our King; Salvation comes now from the Lord,
Our victorious King.
His Holy Name be well ador'd, Salvation surely bring.
Dear Jesus give thy Spirit now,
Thy grace to every Nation,
That hasn't the Lord to whom we bow,
The Author of Salvation.
Dear Jesus unto Thee we cry,
Give us the Preparation,
Turn not away thy tender Eye;
We seek thy true Salvation.
Salvation comes from God we know,
The true and only One;
It's well agreed and certain true,
He gave His only Son.
Lord hear our penitential Cry;
Salvation from above;
It is the Lord that doth supply,
With his Redeeming Love.
Dear Jesus by thy precious Blood,

The World Redemption have:
Salvation now comes from the Lord,
He being thy captive slave.
Dear Jesus let the nations cry,
And all the people say,
Salvation comes from Christ on high,
Haste a Tribunal Day.
We cry as Sinners to the Lord,
Salvation to obtain;
It is firmly fixt his holy Word,
Ye shall not cry in vain.
Dear Jesus unto Thee we cry,
And make our Lamentation:
O let our Prayers ascend on high;
We felt thy Salvation.
Lord turn our dark benighted Souls;
Give us a true Motion,
And let the Hearts of all the World,
Make Christ their Salvation.
Ten Thousand Angels cry to Thee,
Yea louder than an Ocean.
Thou art the Lord, we plainly see;
Thou art the true Salvation.
Now is the day, excepted Times;
The Day of Salvation;
Increase your Faith, do not repine:
Awake ye every Nation.
Lord unto whom now shall we go,
Or seek a safe Abode;
Thou hast the Word of Salvation too
The only Son of God.
Ho! Every one that hunger hath,
Or pineth after me,

Salvation be thy leading Staff,
To set the Sinner free.
Dear Jesus unto Thee we fly;
Depart, depart from Sin,
Salvation doth at length supply,
The Glory of our King.
Come ye Blessed of the Lord,
Salvation greatly given;
O turn your Hearts, accept the Word,
Your Souls are fit for heaven.
Dear Jesus we now turn to Thee,
Salvation to obtain;
Our Hearts and Souls do meet again,
To magnify thy Name.
Come holy Spirit, Heavenly Dove,
The Object of our Care;
Salvation doth increase our Love;
Our hearts hath felt thy fear.
Now Glory be to God on High,
Salvation high and low;
And thus the Soul on Christ rely,
To Heaven surely go.
Come Blessed Jesus, Heavenly Dove,
Accept Repentance here;
Salvation give, with tender Love;
Let us with angels share. Finis.

—JUPITER HAMMON (1711–1806?)

Born into slavery, Jupiter Hammon received an unusually extensive education on the Lloyd Manor Estate, taking advantage of the literature available to him in the Lloyd library and writing his poetry. A preacher to his fellow brethren on the estate, he wrote in broadside poetry and prose styles that were deeply influenced by his religious beliefs.

IN TIMES OF TRIBULATION

Ere Sleep Comes Down to Soothe the Weary Eyes

Ere sleep comes down to soothe the weary eyes,
Which all the day with ceaseless care have sought
The magic gold from which the seeker flies;
Ere dreams put on the cap and gown of thought,
And make the waking world a world of lies,—
Of lies most palpable, uncouth, forlorn,
That say life's full of aches and tears and sighs,—
Oh, how with more than dreams the soul is torn,
Ere sleep comes down to soothe the weary eyes.

Ere sleep comes down to soothe the weary eyes,
How all the griefs and heartaches we have known
Come up like pois'nous vapors that arise
From some base witch's caldron, when the crone,
To work some potent spell, her magic plies.
The past which held its share of bitter pain,
Whose ghost we prayed that Time might exorcise,
Comes up, is lived and suffered o'er again,
Ere sleep comes down to soothe the weary eyes.

Ere sleep comes down to soothe the weary eyes,
What phantoms fill the dimly lighted room;

What ghostly shades in awe-creating guise
Are bodied forth from within the teeming gloom.
What echoes faint of sad and soul-sick cries,
And pangs of vague inexplicable pain
That pay the spirit's ceaseless enterprise,
Come thronging through the chambers of the brain,
Ere sleep comes down to soothe the weary eyes.

—PAUL LAURENCE DUNBAR (1872–1906)

An enormously popular writer during his lifetime, Paul Laurence Dunbar has been praised by James Weldon Johnson as "the first American Negro poet of real literary distinction" and was called "the poet laureate of the Negro race" by civil and women's rights leader Mary Church Terrel.

WE WEAR THE MASK

We wear the mask that grins and lies,
It hides our cheeks and shades our eyes,
This debt we pay to human guile;
With torn and bleeding hearts we smile,
And mouth with myriad subtleties.
Why should the world be overwise,
In counting all our tears and sighs?
Nay, let them only see us, while
We wear the mask.
We smile, but, O great Christ, our cries
To Thee from tortured souls arise.
We sing, but oh, the lay is vile
Beneath our feet, and long the mile;
But let the world dream otherwise,
We wear the mask.

—PAUL LAURENCE DUNBAR (1872–1906)

Although he was the author of many novels and short stories, Paul Laurence Dunbar is best known for writing poetry presented in the "dialect" of Southern blacks.

SELF-PITY

Dear God,

Never let me be plagued by an overwhelming feeling of depression and self-pity—sitting around and allowing thoughts about negative things that have happened to saturate my mind, or becoming incapacitated by wallowing in sorrow for my misfortunes. Let me always know that focusing on myself is not productive; it keeps one from being a vessel for You to work through. Always grant the power to break such train of thought and to stop thinking about myself. Grant me the opportunity to serve someone else or do something for a neighbor. Constantly inspire my mind to see the glory of Your great blessings in my life, not the trivial misfortunes. Knowing You and Your incredible love is my greatest blessing. Please help me to keep the proper perspective on life, and to know the value of sharing it. In Christ's Name.

Amen.

—REVEREND CHESTINA MITCHELL ARCHIBALD

Reverend Archibald comments on the topic of self-pity and self-absorption by saying, "Anyone wrapped in him- or herself makes too small a package to make a difference." Inspiration for the prayer comes from Esther 4:13–14: "Think not with thyself: for if thou altogether holdest thy peace . . . thy father's house shall be destroyed . . ."

RAINSTORM

O Liberator, we bring before you our feelings of woe. You know
   when our defenses are spent.

You see behind our masks. You are acquainted with our weakest places.

Our tears have been numbered by you.

We cry alone.

We cry out loud.

We are even, sometimes, embarrassed by our tears.

Sometimes others are embarrased by our tears.

Sometimes we wish we would not cry at all.

Sometimes we want the tears to burst forth and they won't come.

O Keeper of the soul, on occasion our tears come like a mighty
   downpour.

It moves the body to uncontrollable sobs and heaves.

Momentarily we fear that we may cross over to an emotional never-
   to-return land.

Yet as the rain quiets and lessens and eventually stops, so does our
   tearful outburst.

(Pause)

In the rain the earth is embraced in a sweetness and a freshness and
   a newness.

Likewise, O Comforter, our inner self is emptied and cleansed and
   healed until our next rainstorm.

Till then, we take refuge in our closeness to you.

—REVEREND JULIA A. PRINCE

Reverend Prince comments on the inspiration in writing this prayer: "Drawing
on the complexities of the mourning process, prayerful words of authenticity can
be a healing catalyst. This prayer inspires me because it calls both the person
praying and the one[s] prayed for to a mindful consciousness. This prayerful
declaration hopefully is also one that frees the self."

BAPTISM

Into the furnace let me go alone;
Stay you without the terror of the heat.
I will go naked in—for thus 'tis sweet—
Into the weird depths of the hottest zone.
I will not quiver in the frailest bone,
You will not note a flicker of defeat;
My heart shall tremble not its fate to meet,
Nor mouth give utterance to any moan.
The yawning oven spits forth fiery spears;
Red aspish tongues shout wordlessly my name.
Desire destroys, consumes my mortal fears,
Transforming me into a shape of flame.
I will come out, back to your world of tears,
A stronger soul with a finer frame.

—CLAUDE MCKAY (1890–1948)

Among the published works of Claude McKay are numerous books and essays, three novels, and a collection of poems. His poetry includes lyrics celebrating Christian faith, nature, and love, as well as nostalgic poems about his native rural Jamaica.

A PRAYER OF LAMENTATION

Dear Creator of my life and God of my fears. You are so transcendent to me. So far away and distant from the world that you created. Yet I cannot help but to keep seeking you and longing for your presence. As I go through this period of spiritual alienation in my life I cannot seem to find your resting place nor your place of business. Where do you reside? Where are your ears of compassion? Has your heart of mercy fled before the devastation and the weight of your lost creation? Where art thou?

Persons who say they know Jesus act in ways that are not Christian. The religious right castigate the poor and presume to speak a special word from you. Yet, you do not defend yourself. How do you allow century old wars to rage in Bosnia and the Middle East when you could have interceded long ago? Shepherds mishandle your Word and the Sheep of your pasture suffer, yet you rebuke no one. I cannot bear much more the pictures and images of mutilated and dying children in the Motherland of Africa. The continent that once cradled your son Jesus. The evening news has become a stink and a stench in my nostrils as night after night only death and killings are marched before the eyes of our communities. Then Lord God, to add insult to injury I ask you to protect and bless my son and hours later he is cut down. Has the honor of God answering prayer been taken away? Do you not know? Have we become a shame to you, our creator?

O God! If there is glory in suffering let it come now. If you are speaking through our pain, please speak louder. If you are purging and pruning your people in order to make us more like thee, please just tell us so. For sometimes I feel like it is all in vain. The living, the waiting, the dying, the existing, the praying and the fasting. But I go back to thee, O transcendent being! I keep hearing the echo that reminds me that you are the God of our weary years and you are also the God of our silent tears. In all my suffering I hope in the comfort that you are faithful to your Word. You promised never to leave us alone. In Jesus' name, I trust you to continue to make promises good. I thank you for listening.

Amen.

—REVEREND H. CARLYLE CHURCH, JR.

An accomplished writer, Reverend Church's work has been published in the *Journal and Guide* newspaper, *The Old Dominion University Mace* newspaper, and the *Howard University School of Divinity* newsletter. He has had an editorial published in the *San Francisco Examiner*.

ABANDONED BY GOD

Creator of the worlds and all there is to be and Master of all there is to know, do you truly know my significance and does your knowledge eliminate my insignificance? Where does this overwhelming loneliness come from? Does its very existence, Lord, teach me distance or is it there to create my longing?

Speak, Lord, and I will see, feel, smell, taste, touch and hear. Ahhh, then I inhale and exhale and hear myself say, thank you.
    Amen.

—REVEREND GEORGE S. WILLIS III

Reverend Willis has been a pastor for thirty-eight years at Jones Chapel African Methodist Episcopal Church in Houston, Texas. On the writing of his prayer, he says: "I'm blessed with inspiration, as many of us are, from the Holy Spirit."

WHERE ARE YOU, GOD?
(An Encounter with God)

Jesus, where are you? Do you still work the midnight shift and see the tear-drenched pillows, and hear the painful cries? We know you promised never to leave us, but we cannot seem to find you or feel your omnipresence amidst the sirens and screams. Where are you when distress, disappointments and discontent seem to engulf our communities? Out of the depths of our hearts we come asking that you will grant us wisdom to understand and grace to withstand these times when we do not know if you are among us. We see those who verbally have denied you prosper in health and wealth and we wonder and ask why? O, but in spite of it we will continue to hold on to your promises when all seems futile. We know that you are alive and well and in control. Thank you for the relief and the inner peace we feel now that you have heard how we feel.

—PASTOR JAMES L. DAVIS

James L. Davis is currently pastor at Big Bethel African Methodist Episcopal Church in Atlanta, Georgia. On the writing of this prayer, he says: "The Israelites often cried out to God and African Americans must learn to do the same. God wants to hear from us, and this concept of crying out to God has inspired this prayer."

WHEN I FEEL ABANDONED

Lord: There are times when my prayers
seem to fall on deaf ears

Nothing changes. Problems persist.

I seem to keep repeating the same words
day after day . . . night after night

At times it seems that things only get
worse

Am I praying amiss? Am I somehow hindering
my prayer from being answered?

When I feel this way, I fall back on your
Word, not on how I feel or what I think

I remember past answers, and know that you
hear me

Your ways are not my ways, neither are your
thoughts my thoughts

I claim your promises and rest in them,
giving you praise, for you know best

Thank you for the test!
Amen.

—CHARLIE J. JOHNSON, DOCTOR OF MINISTRY

Currently residing in Sweetwater, Tennessee, Charlie J. Johnson has been a minister since 1947, a pastor for thirty-one years, and is still doing interim work in retirement. On this prayer he says: "When His answers are delayed, I sometimes feel abandoned—but not for long."

A PRAYER AGAINST LONELINESS

O God,

We, as Your children, fashioned in Your very image, are of the greatest value in the Universe. Yet because of the fall of humankind, we feel separated from You and unworthy to even come before Your presence. Lift us out of this abyss of loneliness and despair. Renew our remembrance of Jesus' love and sacrifice. Let us claim our rights as adopted children. Help us continue to follow the precepts of Christ, and to draw closer to Thee. Make us whole as we seek to become worthy sons and daughters. When we experience loneliness, give us the insight to take our attention off of ourselves and to place it on You. No one can feel lonely while his or her mind is stayed on Thee. In the spirit of one who brings perpetual joy.

Amen.

—REVEREND CHESTINA MITCHELL ARCHIBALD

Reverend Archibald was prompted to write this prayer by Psalms 146:5: "Happy is he that hath the God of Jacob for his help, whose hope is in the Lord his God." Loneliness is a problem encountered by each of us at some time, but we must know that God is always with us to protect us, love us, and help us in our times of need.

A Prayer for Companionship

Dear Heavenly Parent,

I am happy with You alone. Yet I pray, that if it be Your will, help me to find a perfect mate. I need Your guidance because I do not want to marry for improper reasons, and I never want to divorce. God, please help me find someone who can complement my character, who can be as committed to You as I am, and who can be my helpmate and soulmate for all time. I pray in Christ's Name.

Amen.

—Reverend Chestina Mitchell Archibald

Reverend Archibald cites Hebrews 13:4 as her motivation to write this prayer: "Marriage is honourable in all, and the bed undefiled." Finding suitable companionship is a problem for many people, but with God's guidance, He may lead them to a loving and compatible mate that is also devoted to His will.

LORD, I'VE BEEN DISAPPOINTED BY SOMEONE

Heavenly Father,

Lord, to be betrayed by someone is such a painful reality. My heart is heavy. A very important promise made to me by someone very close to me was broken, and I feel completely betrayed. I know that more than anyone on earth, You have known betrayal. Those who You created and loved deeply turned their backs on You, killed Your prophets, even Your own Son. Yet, You still love us. Teach me to forget the searing pain of betrayal. Show me how to overcome my hurt feelings. Fill my heart with forgiveness towards him who betrayed me. Let my heart be free from the burden it is under, and let me walk with You in heart and feeling. In Christ's Name.

Amen.

—REVEREND CHESTINA MITCHELL ARCHIBALD

Reverend Archibald was inspired to write this prayer by Psalms 2:12b: "Blessed are all they that put their trust in [God]." When someone lets us down or betrays our trust, God can help us to grant our forgiveness.

POOR RICHARD'S ALMANAC

Lord,
I am tired of hearing about how the rich worked hard to get rich
and how hard the affluent work to stay affluent.
Now that a damned lie, Lord.
If hard work—real labor—
getting up early, and coming home exhausted at night,
is some kind of great virtue and make you affluent,
then, Lord, I've got to tell you the poor would all be rich,
right now.
Only the poor work hard, Lord—
in lousy junkyards, sweatshops, laundries, emptying bed pans—
I see the poor walking and getting on buses to go to work at 6:00 A.M.
Not the affluent.
It's the poor who come home tired and dirty.
The poor don't have two or three hour lunches, or vacations,
or bonuses, or benefits, or decent and safe surroundings to work in.
And when you're poor, Lord,
somebody is watching to see if you're working all the time.
Are you watching too, Lord?
I hope you are.
    Amen.

—ROBERT W. CASTLE, JR.

Born in 1929 in Jersey City, New Jersey, Robert Castle is an Episcopal priest who has also demonstrated a propensity toward writing. He received his education from St. Lawrence University and Berkeley Divinity School in New Haven, Connecticut. This prayer is from his book, *Prayers From the Burned-Out City*, which was written for those residing in inner-cities who face daily the consequences of unemployment, violence, pollution, and poverty.

A PRAYER FOR ENDURANCE

O God, today seems gloomy, yet tomorrow the sun shall come forth in new brilliance. Help us to feel the assurance that the seed we are planting will produce a harvest pleasing in Thy sight.

Give us the patience to wait for the time of threshing before we uncover the seeds we have worked so diligently to plant.

We are tired Lord, renew our strength.
We are ill, grant us Your healing power.
We are confused, grant us wisdom.
When we are lonely, even in the midst of a crowd,
Grant us the awareness of Your omnipresence, that we may know we
    are never alone.
Bless us now, Lord, with power to endure until we feel Your blessed
    assurance. In Your Holy name we pray.
    Amen.

—REVEREND CHESTINA MITCHELL ARCHIBALD

At times the road ahead seems to get steeper, and it becomes more difficult for us to go on. But we are reminded in Isaiah 40:31 that if we open ourselves to God's love, He will give us the will to endure: "They that wait upon the Lord shall renew their strength; they shall mount up with wings as eagles; they shall run, and not be weary; and they shall walk, and not faint."

THE HURDLES ARE TOO CLOSE

Omnipotent God, the hurdles are too close! As soon as I jump over one set of life situations, another set is right before me. I cannot jump them alone.

Help me to see you standing tall and strong next to each hurdle, waiting to lift me high above them all.

When I am weak, teach me to lean on your strength. When my faith wavers, remind me of how you rescued me the last time I was caught in between hurdles of pain, stress, financial disaster and family problems.

It was then that I thought you had abandoned me, then that you showed yourself in small miracles. It is so easy to forget you were the force behind my strength to climb over the hurdles of two months ago, because all I can see is the present obstacles, and so I easily forget your help of ages past. Lord, I know you have never left me, it is my faith that has wavered. Strengthen me to know that I am not alone and remove the hurdles of hindrances, I pray.

—PASTOR JAMES L. DAVIS

Pastor Davis explains the theme of this prayer: "Life's circumstances are so similar to hurdles. Watching an athlete jump them and try to balance and adjust to face the next inspired this prayer. When the hurdles are so close, we feel that God is not near."

A PRAYER FOR STRENGTH IN TIMES OF DESPAIR

Our eternal Father of all mercy and giver of all grace, we call upon you to come in this time of weakness and deliver us from our trials. We acknowledge, O Lord, that the trials we face in life today, though they be burdensome to us, they are not beyond your reach. For through your spirit we trust all things will work for good for those who truly love you. Comfort our distress and the anxiety of our despair; help us to find courage and faith to endure our hardships and trials. Yet within our trials show us how to come closer to you. Let us find refuge in your comfort and delight in our hope. In thee do we put our trust and in the name of Jesus do we pray.

Amen.

—REVEREND DR. LYNN HARGROW

Reverend Hargrow, pastor at St. Matthew's Christian Methodist Episcopal Church in Wichita, Kansas, says: "This is a prayer that I ask for myself as I labor in ministry as a pastor and Christian educator. I often run into frustrations and situations of despair in which I feel nothing is happening or that I am just running and not getting anywhere. Things may not always go the way I think they should, but I have to keep laboring until God reveals the answers. This is a prayer of strength that God will help me look beyond my feelings of despair."

GOD OF OUR WEARY YEARS

God of our weary years,
God of our silent,
Thou who hast brought us thus far on the way.

Thou who hast by Thy might
led us into the light,
Keep us forever in the path, we pray;

Lest our feet stray from the places, our God, where we met
Thee,
Lest our hearts drunk with the wine of the world, we forget
Thee.

Shadowed beneath Thy hand,
May we forever stand,
True to our God, true to our native land!

—JAMES WELDON JOHNSON (1871–1938)

In addition to serving as a consul to Venezuela and Nicaragua between 1906 and 1912, James Weldon Johnson also represented the Institute on Pacific Relations held in Kyoto, Japan. His powerful poetic, philosophical, critical, and historical writings coincide with his belief that a people's true mark on civilization was based on their literary contributions.

ABOUT SLAVERY AND FREEDOM
From *Narrative of the Life of Frederick Douglass* (1845)

Douglass's lamentation on slavery is historically significant and continues to be relevant to those who feel shackled to heavy burdens and difficult situations. Writing about his time of bondage in Maryland, Frederick Douglass spoke of watching sailboats gliding along Chesapeake Bay from his master's estate:

> The sight of these always affected me powerfully. My thoughts would compel utterance; and there, with no audience but the Almighty, I would pour out my soul's complaint, in my rude way, with an apostrophe to the moving multitude of ships:
>
> You are loosed from your moorings, and are free; I am fast in my chains, and am a slave! You move merrily before the gentle gale, and I sadly before the bloody whip! You are freedom's swift-winged angels, that fly round the world; I am confined in bands of iron! Oh that I were free! O, that I were on one of your gallant decks, and under your protecting wing! Alas! betwixt me and you, the turbid waters roll. Go on, go on. O that I could also go! Could I but swim! If I could fly! O, why was I born a man, of whom to make a brute! The glad ship is gone; she hides in the dim distance. I am left in the hottest hell of unending slavery. O God, save me! God deliver me! Let me be free! Is there any God? Why am I slave? I will run away. I will not stand it. Get caught, or get clear, I'll try it. I had as well die with ague as the fever. I have only one life to lose. I had as well be killed running as die standing. Only think of it; one hundred miles straight north, and I am free! Try it? Yes! God helping me, I will.

—FREDERICK DOUGLASS (1817–1895)

Born a slave in Baltimore, Maryland, Frederick Douglass escaped from slavery in 1838 and went on to become one of the most influential figures in African American history. During his work for social reform and the abolition of slavery, he began speaking out publicly, soon drawing large audiences due to his natural ability as a speaker. He served as an enlistment officer in the Civil War, encouraging Lincoln toward emancipation. After the war, he held various government positions, including U.S. marshal for the District of Columbia and minister to Haiti.

WHEN I FEEL THREATENED

Lord, I am so glad I know You. It never ceases to amaze me that threatened people are often wealthy, successful, good-looking, and seemingly brimming with confidence. Many people judge their value by them. Spiritual value is often ridiculed or belittled. I pray to be able to embody a pure and unselfish confidence based on the fact that I am Your loyal and beloved child. I pray never to let false greatness in others threaten my own feeling of contentment. I pray that the values that I possess as Your child can give me a feeling of ownership and love for all things and shield me from attempts to undermine my strength and credibility. When I feel threatened and withdrawn, I cannot be a vessel for Your love and truth. Please help me to remember not only who I am and what I possess, but whose I am, thus all things are mine. In Christ's Name, I pray.

Amen.

—REVEREND CHESTINA MITCHELL ARCHIBALD

The theme of this prayer is illustrated in 1 Peter 2:23: "When he suffered, he threatened not; but committed himself to him that judgeth righteously." The love we know God feels for us can help us to be strong when we might otherwise feel intimidated.

LORD, PROTECT ME FROM DANGER

O Lord, our God, how excellent is Thy name. God we are grateful for Your protection. You are our refuge and our strength and our help in times of trouble. You are the One who shields us from the fiery darts of danger. The hateful acts of injustice, persecution, criticism, condemnation and malice have no power over us. In the midnight of our terror, God we thank You for the calm assurance of knowing that we do not have to be afraid. You have promised to deliver us and deliverance is certain. We rest in the comfort of Your love.

Amen.

—REVEREND YVONNE HOWZE

In addition to being cochairman of a community planning group on HIV/AIDS, Reverend Howze is also director of education for the AIDS Task Force for Alabama. In writing this prayer, she was inspired by Psalms 91:10: "There is no evil befall thee, neither shall any plague come nigh thy dwelling."

A Prayer for Peace of Mind

Dear God of Peace and Calmness,

My heart is heavy with worry. May I be forever mindful that You are in charge and that worry is antithetical to faith. Take my worry from me and liberate my heart. Lord, admittedly, there are times when my faith gets weak. At those times, help me to pull on my confidence in Thee. Help me not to just hope because of things You will do in the future, but help me to recall Your faithful acts in the past. I know that You are the same yesterday, today, and tomorrow, and with this assurance I now rest.

Amen.

—Reverend Chestina Mitchell Archibald

Reverend Archibald was influenced by Psalms 37:11 in the writing of this prayer: "The meek shall inherit the earth; and shall delight themselves in the abundance of peace." The prayer reminds us that faith in God is the key to a calm spirit and peaceful heart.

LORD, DELIVER US FROM FEAR

O God, our help in ages past, our hope in years to come, our shelter from the stormy blast and our eternal home. Dear sheltering spirit, we dare not doubt a God who has been our only help in the time of need in all of our troublesome yesteryears. So at this time we approach thy throne of grace with boldness and with our most urgent needs. Grant us deliverance from the fear and evil that is before us now. Fulfill now to us the promise of your word, "Fear not, for I will never leave you, nor forsake you." You are our great deliverer and our strong tower of defense. As the world rages against us we shall continue to trust in your promises and the might of your glory. We believe that our deliverance has come now. In the name of Jesus Christ, we proudly thank you for your care and the answer to our request.

Amen.

—REVEREND H. CARLYLE CHURCH, JR.

Reverend Church currently serves as a member of the Ph.D. Task Force at the Howard University School of Divinity in Washington, D.C. He is also a member of *Who's Who in American Colleges and Universities.*

HOPE

O Loving and Holy God:
It's awfully dark in here because I'm getting tired of trying.
People in the church are talking about me.
My friends are hard to find when my heart seems so low.
Work is competitive and full of jealousy.
But I won't give up becuase you have put a picture of your will in
    my heart.
You are my God and I won't quit because you cannot fail. And when
    I think about being on your
team, working for your purpose, I get energized again and even my
    problems lift me.

Lord God, when I think about how you've been with me through
    tough times in the past I feel
like going on . . .
I know that there will be days of tests in the future but that is where
    you've asked me to go.
Help me, O God, to praise you, the source of my strength. It is such
    a blessing to be in your
presence! I'm feeling better already. I'm going on. Thank you, God,
    for the gift of hope.
    Amen.

—JAMES KING

James King is director of the Conference Council Office of the United Methodist
Church in Nashville, Tennessee. An impressive coordinator, he organizes programs for more than four hundred churches.

ON SEEKING THE LORD'S PATH

CREATE IN ME A TENDER, LOVING HEART

You, God of love, created all things. Your love for us is deep, wide, and greater than human understanding. I look at the insect world and the animal kingdom with awe and trembling. The ways in which You have equipped plants and animals to reproduce are neverending. How much more did You invest in humans? How much more do You love us? You gave us dominion over all things, yet sin makes us want to rule. Do You shed tears for Your lost sons and daughters? Do You long for the sweet embrace of love from pure spirit? Create in me, Lord, a clean heart, a tender spirit, and a mind to love Thee, that I may demonstrate Your tender and complete love for us all. In Christ's Name.

Amen.

—REVEREND CHESTINA MITCHELL ARCHIBALD

Reverend Archibald was influenced by Psalms 10:17 when writing this prayer: "Lord, thou hast heard the desire of the humble: thou wilt prepare their heart, thou wilt cause thine ear to hear." The creation of all things on Earth is living proof of the glorious omnipotence of God.

FOR UNDERSTANDING TRUE SUCCESS

Dear God, Ruler of All Creation,

Many are rich in houses and land. Others work hard every day and it seems like their work is in vain; they never seem to get ahead. Lord, what is success? How can one be successful? Is success to be found in the type of house one has or the amount of money one can amass? Who do You consider successful? Please, God, help us know what success is for Your children. No one is a complete failure who knows You. However, Lord, why is it that many have to struggle from day to day? Is there something one can do to be greater in Your eyes? Biblical teachings say he who shall be great must be the servant of all. Is the reward to be only spiritual? Please God, help me see clearly and push me to the success which You will for me. In Christ's name.

Amen.

—REVEREND CHESTINA MITCHELL ARCHIBALD

Inspiration for this prayer was found in Malachi 3:10: "Bring ye all the tithes into the Storehouse, that there may be meat in thine house, and prove me now herewith, saith the Lord of hosts, if I will not open you the windows of heaven and pour you a blessing, that there shall not be room enough to receive it."

A PRAYER FOR SUCCESS

Lord, give me a goal. For we know it must be borne in mind that the tragedy of life doesn't lie in not reaching your goal. The tragedy lies in having no goal to reach. It isn't a calamity to die with dreams unfulfilled but it is a calamity not to dream! It is not a disaster to be unable to capture your ideal, but it is a disaster to have no ideal to capture. It is not a disgrace not to reach the stars, but it is a disgrace to have no stars to reach for. For we know not failure, but low aim is sin.

Amen.

—REVEREND BENJAMIN E. MAYS (1895–1984)

President of Morehouse College from 1940 until 1967, Reverend Mays was also a prominent civil rights leader. Among many other important events in his life, he delivered the eulogy at Martin Luther King, Jr.'s funeral.

LOYALTY TO GOD

Almighty and Trustworthy God, to You we pray. We thank You for being a God in whom we can depend. A God who will never leave us; never fail nor forsake us. We thank You, Lord, that we can stand with a firm assurance that everything is going to be alright. We know this is true because You are God. You are truth. Lord, help us to be loyal to one another, and by this we show our allegiance to You. Help us to be servants mindful of Your Omnipotence, Omnipresence, and Omniscience. O Lord, we ask this in the name of Your beloved son, Jesus the Christ.

Amen.

—REVEREND CHESTINA MITCHELL ARCHIBALD

We are reminded in Malachi 4:2–3 of the great privileges given God's loyal followers: ". . . unto you that fear my name shall the sun of righteousness arise with healing in his wings . . . and shall tread down the wicked: for they shall be like ashes under the soles of your feet . . ." Unwavering faith ensures that anything can be accomplished with God's love, and that His strength can help overcome any obstacle.

AFFIRMATION OF GOD'S PRESENCE

God, you are near to us. We praise you for your steadfastness and abiding presence. In the seasons of living, we all have periods where changes bring feelings of anguish, remorse and sorrow. It does not discriminate. Rich ones, poor ones, tall ones, short ones, the known and the unknown, the churched and the unchurched, the powerful, the powerless, the popular, the unpopular and the seemingly worthless ones, all belong to You. You are the all-wise God. We can trust that to each and every one of us, You will give the particular listening and desired healing. Help us to accept ourselves. Help us to accept the differences in our grieving styles and manifestations. Help us not to judge another until we have dared to come in empathy. Empower us to give to others the comfort we ourselves have received. Keep us from destructive elements of self-pity. Give us the courage to embrace the necessary changes that will move us beyond brokenness to wholeness so that we can once again laugh, love and lift. Stay near to us, O Protector, lest we become blinded by our seeming self-sufficiency.

—REVEREND JULIA A. PRINCE

Reverend Prince explains the theme of her prayer: "Mourning is part of living—it comes with the gift of life. This prayer is inspired by the theology of 'We help others, we help ourselves.' We share, support, and pray for one another. Regardless of our particular mourning phase, people of faith accept that God is present."

HELP ME RECOGNIZE TRUTH

O God of Truth,

Jesus said He was the way, the truth, and the life. Yet many people did not believe Him. Today, many still don't believe. To the people of His day, His words were shocking and seemed to be blasphemous. Many religious leaders feared Him because if their followers left them to follow Jesus, they would lose their high positions. Jesus lamented the disbelief of those who heard Him and even proclaimed it was Your will for them to believe in Him who You had sent. Yet, His words fell on deaf ears. His very life was taken before the spiritual eyes and ears of many could be healed. Lord, I pray that my spiritual eyes and ears may be finely tuned to Your heart and will and that I can recognize what is true and what is false in this world of dangerous illusions. Please protect me from becoming like those who rejected and persecuted our Lord. I want to participate in the fulfillment of Your will. Fill my mind with a clear understanding of Your holy word.

Many argue that truth is relative, but I believe You are our God and You created us with a purpose. I believe You are steadfast and thus never wavered from Your original plan. Therefore, the principles by which You created are absolute and unchanging. Lord, show us our role in helping to bring about a world of love and harmony where Your truth is revealed. Open our minds and hearts to receive Your word, Your truth, that we might be vessels in Your service. In Christ's Name.

    Amen.

—REVEREND CHESTINA MITCHELL ARCHIBALD

The writing of this prayer was inspired by John 14:6: "Jesus saith . . . I am the way, the truth, and the life, no man cometh unto the Father, but by me." The mystery of God is difficult for us to understand, but we know He is the Truth as we witness each day the miracles and gifts He has given to us.

A PRAYER FOR WISDOM

O Lord our God, reveal to us your heart and character so that we in turn will yield our hearts minds and wills to obey your commands. It is in listening and hearing from you that we can set our hearts to obey your commands and follow your instructions.

We recognize that our craving for wisdom, deliverance, and freedom can only be fulfilled in you, so grant us the patience to listen to your wisdom and the courage to apply our minds to your knowledge. Our cry in this hour is "that we may know you." We understand that to "know you" is a lifelong process. A lifelong process of seeking after you and a lifelong process of searching for the good in life. It is only by so doing that we can come to know you, the eternal One, the supplier of wisdom, insight, and knowledge.

Your help is readily available and granted upon request to those who seek after you. Grant us the grace of honesty because you are a shield to those who live honestly. You are our lifeguard and protection from those who act wickedly toward us. Your light, O God, gives us a clear path to follow and when we walk in that path of life our personhood is solidified (established), our joy complete, we survive our trials, and our wicked enemies are destroyed before our eyes. These great acts we will not forget.

—DR. JOHN J. FINN

Dr. Finn is pastor and founder of Faith, Hope and Love Fellowship Church in Nashville, Tennessee. He and his wife, copastor Judith J. Finn, are parents to six children.

A PRAYER SEEKING WISDOM

O God of King Solomon, Harriet Tubman, Sojourner Truth, Ida B. Wells, and Mary McLeod Bethune, to You we pray. We have seen through these lives how You are a granter of knowledge and wisdom. Like these, we come to You as humble as we know how, acknowledging our ignorance. We come knowing that true knowledge and wisdom can only come as a gift from You. Lord, grant us that gift and help us demonstrate wisdom in our daily affairs, so that You are glorified. In the name of Jesus the Christ we pray.

Amen.

—REVEREND CHESTINA MITCHELL ARCHIBALD

The theme of this prayer is found in Psalms 3:13: "Happy is the [person] that findeth wisdom, and . . . getteth understanding." In order to thank God for the wonderful gifts of knowledge and wisdom He has given us, we must use these gifts in ways that will please Him and show Him our infinite appreciation.

PRAYER FOR INSPIRATION

Father, may I be filled with the knowledge of your will in all wisdom and spiritual understanding; that I may walk fully pleasing, being fruitful in every good work, and increasing the knowledge of God. Strengthened with all might, according to His glorious power, unto all patience and long-suffering with joyfulness. Giving thanks unto the Father, who has qualified me to be a partaker of the inheritance of the saints in light. He has delivered me from the power of darkness and conveyed me into the kingdom of the Son of His love, in whom I have redemption through His blood, even the forgiveness of sins. He is the image of the invisible God, the first born over all creation.

—KIM FIELDS FREEMAN

Actress Kim Fields Freeman is best known for her work on television in the long-running series *The Facts of Life* and, most recently, on the situation comedy *Living Single*. She was inspired to write this prayer by Colossians 1:9: "And so . . . we have not ceased to pray for you, asking that you may be filled with the knowledge of His will."

A PRAYER ON HONESTY

Our heavenly Father, teach us this night and forever to remember that Thou hatest a lie, for a lie is a pitiable, degrading and dangerous thing. Dangerous to a universe whose foundations are God's Truth, degrading to young growing characters which should be open, honest and sincere; and pitiable for boys and girls like these who ought to despise deception and deceit. Create in us, O God, that high sense of honor and self-respect which will suffer disgrace and punishment rather than stoop to a falsehood. [Well we know, our Father, that among us here, it is not so much the great deceptions as it is the little lies, the petty fibbing that hurts—things too small for the world's true workers to soil their souls with.] Deliver us from tattlers, tale-bearers and liars. Teach us that silence may save us from such things but that a lie can never save a human soul from its own damnation and the world's disgust. [We live in the midst of lies, O God. Slavery was a lie and much of this problem of races is a mass of lies. But may we as Christians and as men rise above our surroundings and become true and honest men and women, abhorring whatsoever worketh abomination or maketh a lie.]

Amen.

—W. E. B. DU BOIS (1868–1963)

After he migrated to Africa in 1961, W. E. B. Du Bois became editor-in-chief of the *Encyclopedia Africana*. He died in Ghana in 1963 at age ninety-five, leaving behind a legacy of outstanding accomplishments.

Prayer for a Humble Heart

During the picking season my grandmother would get out of bed at four o'clock (she never used an alarm clock) and creak down to her knees and chant in a sleep-filled voice, "Our Father, thank you for letting me see this New Day. Thank you that you didn't allow the bed I lay on last night be my cooling board, nor my blanket my winding sheet. Guide my feet this day along the straight and narrow, and help me to put a bridle on my tongue. Bless this house and everybody in it. Thank you, in the name of your son, Jesus Christ, Amen."

—Maya Angelou

Best known as a poet-author, Maya Angelou has had an extremely successful and varied career, which has encompassed acting, singing, and dancing. She was also heavily involved in the civil rights movement, serving as the northern coordinator for Martin Luther King, Jr.'s Southern Christian Leadership Conference in 1959. In January 1993, she became the first woman and the first African American to read her work at a presidential inauguration. This prayer comes from *I Know Why the Caged Bird Sings* (1970), an autobiographical account of her youth and her most critically acclaimed work.

A PRAYER OF HUMILITY

Father God,
I humbly bow before thee. Thank you for your tender mercies. For I can do nothing without you. You are my hope, my love, my joy, my strength. Yet, I can do all things through you. Forgive me, when I struggle uselessly and fall short of your expectations of me. When human challenges come my way, thank you for you are my fortress and my assurance. Keep me forever in the path of righteousness for you are my way, truth and life. I thank you for all of my needs met in whatever form or manifestations required. You are my banker, lawyer, teacher, my mother and my father and all is well because I have chosen to rest in thee.

Amen.

—REVEREND CLAUDETTE THOMPSON CALLAWAY

Reverend Claudette Thompson Callaway is a minister in Detroit, Michigan. In this prayer she emphasizes the importance of simply praising God. It is fulfilling and reassuring to offer thanks and praise without asking for blessing in return, and even this thankfulness is presented with complete humility.

A Prayer

Our Father, grant us the power to transcend selfishness with love, resentment with gratitude and ill-will with understanding.

Amen.

—MARY McLEOD BETHUNE (1875–1955)

During her remarkable life, Mary McLeod Bethune let her drive and determination lead her from her humble beginnings all the way to becoming a college president and adviser to the president of the United States. Another notable event in her life was attending the conference in San Francisco, as a representative of the U.S. State Department, which established the United Nations.

A PRAYER DECRYING VANITY

"Vanity, vanity, Lord all is vanity."

God of Beauty and God of Love,
In this world, many base the value of a person on outward appearances, material possessions and other accomplishments applauded by society. This often creates an atmosphere which dwarfs the spirits. I pray sincerely that every person can feel immeasurable value as Your child as they tap into the resources that come only from knowing You. Physical beauty, You have given us all a measure, yet it fades. The spirit remains forever. Therefore, let us form our spirits with great care, not relying on only externals to shape our reality. Lest we will find ourselves lost and alone. Even those of us who are most beautiful physically will soon see age wash it away. I pray for the strength to avoid vanity and to practice true spiritual laws in my daily life. In Christ's Name.

    Amen.

—REVEREND CHESTINA MITCHELL ARCHIBALD

Reverend Archibald contemplated Psalms 24:3–4 when writing this prayer: "Who shall ascend the hill of the Lord? Or who shall stand in his holy place? He that hath clean hands, and a pure heart; who hath not lifted up his soul unto vanity, nor sworn deceitfully." Instead of working on perfecting our physical beauty, God wants us to spend time improving our inner selves.

LORD, HELP ME RESPECT OTHERS

1. Thy presence why withdraw'st, Lord?
Why hid'st thou now thy face,
When dismal times of deep distress
Call for thy wonted grace?

2. The wicked, swell'd with lawless pride,
Have made the poor their prey;
O let them fall by those designs
Which they for others lay.

3. For straight they triumph, if success
Their thriving crimes attend;
And sordid wretches, whom God hates,
Perversely they commend.

4. To own a pow'r above themselves
Their haughty pride disdains;
And, therefore, in their stubborn mind
No thought of God remains.

5. Oppressive methods they pursue
And all their foes they slight;
Because thy judgments, unobserv'd,
Are far above their sight.

6. They fondly think their prosp'rous state
Shall unmolested be;
They think their vain design shall thrive,
For all misfortunes free.

7. Vain and deceitful is their speech,
With curses fill'd, and lies;
By which the mischief of their heart
They study to disguise.

8. Near public roads they lie conceal'd
And all their art employ,
The innocent and poor at once
To rifle and destroy.

9. Not lions, crouching in their dens,
Surprise their heedless prey
With greater cunning, or express
More savage rage than they.

10. Sometimes they act the harmless man,
And modest looks they wear;
That so deceiv'd the poor may less
Their sudden onset fear.

PART II

11. For, God, they think, no notice takes,
Of their unrighteous deeds;
He never minds the suff'ring poor,
Nor their oppression heeds.

12. But thou, O Lord, at length arise,
Stretch forth thy mighty arm,
And, by greatness of thy pow'r,
Defend the poor from harm.

13. No longer let the wicked vaunt,
And, proudly boasting, say
"Tush, God regards not what we do;
He never will repay."

This prayer was referred to by David Walker in his famous *Appeal*, the powerful call to arms for the abolitionist movement. The *Appeal* was organized into four sections that dealt with slavery, ignorance, Christianity, and colonization. In his writing, Walker simultaneously criticized America's policies towards blacks and encouraged African Americans to empower themselves and to be proud of who they were.

A Prayer on Respect

Lord, teach me to respect other people and the way they live and the things they believe. Help me to never be cruel. Help me to trust other people and to respect their freedom to be different, and Lord, teach me to respect myself before I demand respect from others.

Amen.

—Reverend Chestina Mitchell Archibald

Reverend Archibald cites Romans 2:11 as helping to inspire her to write this prayer: "For there is no respect of persons with God." Respect for others is crucial in trying to live life according to God's will.

A Prayer for Constructive Waiting

Lord, hurry and teach me patience, so that anxiety will not permeate my being, and frustration will not be my constant state. Help me learn to use long periods of waiting constructively, organizing tasks to be fulfilled later or planning for days ahead. More importantly, let me learn to be calm and spend this time in quiet meditation with Thee. Help me block out the busyness about me. Let me go into the closed closets of my own mind that I may emerge refreshed. As I recall Your word: "Ye that wait upon the Lord shall renew His strength." I now, Lord, use this time to wait on Thee.

Amen.

—Reverend Chestina Mitchell Archibald

It is easy in today's world to become impatient when we are forced to wait—however, God can help us be more patient and to use the time we wait valuably. This prayer is based on Galatians 5:5: "For we through the Spirit wait for the hope of righteousness by faith."

LORD, HELP ME TO BE TRUSTWORTHY

Lord, let me put trust in only You, for all else wavers and is inconsistent. You are my solid rock—Your word and purpose never change. I look only toward You for direction. Guide me in my relationships to others. May I always be one who can be trusted by all. May I interact in harmony, never breaking a trust or doing anything to cause heartache. I pray that others can feel safe when approaching me. Let my life and light so shine in the brightest sense. Let me never accidentally hurt another in a careless fashion. May sincerity in all of my dealings be my trademark. In Christ's Name.

Amen.

—REVEREND CHESTINA MITCHELL ARCHIBALD

Reverend Archibald found inspiration from 2 Corinthians 12:6 in writing this prayer: "The law of truth was in his mouth, and iniquity was not found in his lips: he walked with me in peace of equity, and did not turn away from iniquity." Living life according to God's will means honoring His desire for truth and honesty, and refraining from causing pain to others.

A PRAYER FOR USEFULNESS

God grant us the desire to be useful—to look not upon ourselves simply as centers of pleasure and good, but rather as instruments in Thy hands for helping and cheering and doing. We would not forget, O God, that great and wonderful as this Thy world is, it holds but dross and disappointment for them that seek simply to enjoy it. Only to those who seek life in the happiness of human souls, and in the service of those whom Thou hast builded in Thine own image— only then and to them are the secret treasures of the world revealed. This is the lesson of life. May we learn it.

Amen.

—W. E. B. DU BOIS (1868–1963)

One of the most influential African Americans of the twentieth century, William Edward Burghardt Du Bois was an outstanding critic, scholar, author, editor, and civil rights leader. Among his exceptional accomplishments, he was one of the founding fathers of the National Association for the Advancement of Colored People (NAACP).

GOD, HELP ME TO BE USEFUL TO YOU AND OTHERS

It never ceases to amaze me, God, that You in Your infinite wisdom have chosen me to be an instrument in Your service here on earth. You are simply magnificent, and I am glad I said, "Here am I Lord— send me."

Yet it breaks my heart to see Your beloved children—in whom You have created unbridled potential—become useless, without direction or purpose. We live below our privileges and go in opposite directions from the purpose for which You created us. Help us who are throwing our gifts away in riotous living to arise and return to You, our creator. Only then can we be what You have called us to be. In Thy holy name, we pray.

    Amen.

—REVEREND CHESTINA MITCHELL ARCHIBALD

Reverend Archibald found inspiration for writing this prayer in I Timothy 4:14a: "Neglect not the gift that is in thee . . ." We each have special gifts that God has given us, and by looking to Him for direction, we can utilize these gifts in such a way that will please Him and show Him our humble gratitude.

LORD, LET ME BE A WITNESS TO YOUR WORD

Let me not keep silent in a world that needs to hear a prophetic voice. Give utterance to my words, O Lord, that I might be a witness to Your holy name. Fill my heart with joy and love until my actions speak louder than my best words. Let those around me see You in me. As I go through my everyday duties, I pray not to forget You. May there be opportunities each day for me to share my knowledge and love for You, witnessing to Your abundant love, mercy, hope, and will. Lord, You are my inspiration. Please guide me to give my blessings of a happy heart and a cheerful countenance away, making room for more to flow in and through me. In Christ's Name.

Amen.

—REVEREND CHESTINA MITCHELL ARCHIBALD

This prayer was inspired by Ecclesiastes 2:26: "For God giveth to him that is good in his sight, wisdom, and knowledge, and joy . . ." By opening yourself to God's word, you can become a vessel for His spirit, living life by spreading His love.

Prayers for the Community

If my people which are called by my name, shall humble
themselves, and pray, and seek my face, and turn from their
wicked ways, then will I hear from heaven, and will forgive
their sin, and will heal their land.

2 CHRONICLES 7:14

LORD, HELP ME TO SERVE OTHERS IN YOUR NAME

Grant, I beseech Thee, O God, humility of spirit.

I desire to live for the sake of others, but it is not always easy to understand which choices are inherently self-centered and which are altruistic. God, let me not do good works for others in order to bring glory to myself. Let all glory be to You, O God. In Christ's name.

    Amen.

—REVEREND CHESTINA MITCHELL ARCHIBALD

Helping others is a noble goal, but we must remember that the true purpose behind serving others is to glorify God. Otherwise, our own desires may interfere, sometimes in unforeseen ways.

A Prayer on Volunteering

O Great and Giving God,

How often my heart is centered on my own needs and desires. You who art love gave your only begotten son for the sake of others. All of creation is called to give for the sake of others. My spirit longs to fulfill itself by giving unselfishly, yet my actions are blocked by selfishness. Clear away the barriers that keep me from giving to others. Grant me spiritual liberation. Allow me to see the needs of others and respond without thought of reward. Help me to volunteer my time and talents, and willingly share my treasure. Strengthen me in my own faith, so that others may be inspired, and touched by You through me. In Christ's Name.

Amen.

—Reverend Chestina Mitchell Archibald

True greatness, like the spirit of God, is achieved through humble generosity. Through gentleness, one becomes strong. "That all the peoples of the earth may know the hand of the Lord, that it is mighty . . ." (Joshua 4:24).

A PRAYER ON SERVICE

Great God of the Universe,

Jesus demonstrated the art of servitude. If I am to follow in His footsteps, then I also must adopt the posture that my life should be a life of service to others, rather than a life in which I expect others to serve me. Please inspire me to see how I can live a life of service. May my sacrifice help others come closer to You. Help me gain an understanding of the life of Christ and His nature of service. You are the Creator of all things. You brought all things into existence. You know from whence I have come and where I am going. Lord, I pray that you fill me with joy in serving others. Let my service not be for show, form, or fashion to this world, but to please You, the true and living God. In Christ's Name.

Amen.

—REVEREND CHESTINA MITCHELL ARCHIBALD

Too often our desire is to have God bless us rather than work through us to bless others. Jesus said, "For I came . . . not to do mine own will, but the will of Him that sent me" (John 6:38).

PRAYER FOR A CHURCH

O God, at our worship services, we come thanking you for Jesus, who has saved us from spiritual bankruptcy. When we had over-drawn our checking account of moral and legal righteousness and had no collateral for redemption, Jesus invested the cash flow of His blood to cleanse the stain of our depleted account, and His mercy prevented the requirements of justice from closing our spiritual banking account in time and for eternity. We come thanking you for the Holy Spirit which appreciates the ticker tape of our spiritual investments so that no Dow Jones Average of worldly values will depreciate the power of communing with you.

For he was burdened and bereaved in our midst, for the sick and suffering, for the prisoners in detention, for the abused, confused, and misused, for the helpless and hopeless, for those who are weak and weary, commune with us at our table. Commune with us so that our souls, suffering from malnutrition, will renew their strength from the nutrition of feasting at your table. And may the economics of heaven invade this recessionary earth with blessings that will overflow our capacity to receive them. This we pray in Jesus's name. Amen.

—DR. J. ALFRED SMITH, SR.

Dr. Smith is currently senior pastor of Allen Temple Baptist Church in Oakland, California, and professor of Christian ministry at The American Baptist Seminary of the West and the Graduate Theological Union of Berkeley. He is also visiting professor at Fuller Theological Seminary.

A PRAYER ON TITHING

Lord God Almighty,

In Your Word You have directed us to give one tenth of our earnings to You. You amplified this meaning in the parable where the rich man gives a lot, and the poor woman gives just a pittance—yet it was clear that the poor woman gave from her heart when she had little, but the rich man gave what was easy for him to give. Lord, I know that when we tithe, You see the heart and not the amount. Please guide us to give willingly, gladly, and joyously, giving not only our tithes of money, but our talents and time as well. God, truly we can never give enough to repay Your precious gift of life and the offering of Your Son, Jesus, on the cross. I pray now for sincere hearts at the time of offering.

Amen.

—REVEREND CHESTINA MITCHELL ARCHIBALD

Sharing our money, as well as our helping hands, is a longstanding biblical tradition. But giving with a generous heart enables us to experience the joy of giving—an added blessing. "And thither ye shall bring your burnt offerings, and your sacrifices, and your tithes, and leave offerings of your hand, and your vows, and your freewill offerings, and the firstlings of your herds and of your flocks: And there ye shall eat before the Lord your God, and ye shall rejoice in all that you put your hand unto . . ." (Deuteronomy 12:6–7).

ON TITHING MORE THAN MONEY

Lord, You have clearly set before us the directive to give first one tenth of all our earnings to You. Lord, I have followed Your directive and have been blessed by obeying Your law. Help me now, Lord, to be steadfast in gaining as much as I can, so that I can do as much good as I can, for as many people as I can, as long as I shall live.

Amen.

—REVEREND CHESTINA MITCHELL ARCHIBALD

When we work hard in a spirit of openness and giving, the abundance of the universe comes to us in return. Therefore, labor itself is part of all that we offer to God and the world. "Thou shalt truly tithe all the increase of thy seed . . ." (Deuteronomy 14:22).

A PRAYER ON FREEDOM

Free at last, free at last,
Thank God Almighty, I'm free at last.

I was a sinner just like you,
Thank God Almighty, I'm free at last;
I prayed and mourned till I came through,
Thank God Almighty, I'm free at last.

I never shall forget that day,
Thank God Almighty I'm free at last;
When Jesus washed my sins away,
Thank God Almighty I'm free at last.

The very time I thought I was lost,
Thank God Almighty, I'm free at last;
My dungeon shook and my chains fell off,
Thank God Almighty, I'm free at last.

This is religion, I do know,
Thank God Almighty, I'm free at last;
For I never felt such a love before,
Thank God Almighty, I'm free at last.

—TRADITIONAL PRAYER

This traditional prayer demonstrates the gratitude and appreciation we offer to God for the liberty he has given us all. Many people have heard its lines echoed in the famous speech given by Reverend Martin Luther King, Jr.

PRAYER AGAINST ANTIPATHY

O Gracious and Almighty God, You who art all knowing, ever loving and mindful of all that concerns your creatures. Lord, you know we are in a world that is corrupt and invaded by evilness. Protect us and give us power to overcome the evil one. Break the spell of antipathy so that hatred may be turned to love, dislikes to likes, and disgust to acceptance.

Lord, protect my children and my children's children and children everywhere from this ugliness. In the mighty name of Jesus the Christ, we pray.

Amen.

—REVEREND LORRAINE M. DELILLE

Reverend DeLille, of San Dimas, California, was inspired to write this prayer after contemplating the unfortunate excess of hostility in the world today. She based this prayer on the way we can use the power given to us by God to fight to eradicate evil, and the importance of letting the Holy Spirit be our teacher.

A Prayer for Oppression

O Good and Gracious God,
In the midst of time when the force of evil would seem to hold sway
It is so refreshing to be touched by the awareness of Your presence.

In so many simple ways, You allow us to encounter those things
which seem to correct the distorted and fragmented realities that too
often capture our conscience.

When the hue of our complexion is disparaged by some,
You allow us to see a surface of rich mahogany.
When the texture of our hair is maligned,
You allow us to touch a tapestry of fine wool.
When the contour of our anatomy is looked upon with disdain,
You allow us to see statues of great beauty.
When the fullness of our features is belittled,
You allow us to see the handiwork of God.

Let us forever be mindful that all You have done, You have done
    well,
And for this we are most grateful.
In the name of the most high God we pray.
    Amen.

—Reverend Edwin Sanders

Reverend Sanders is currently serving as pastor of the Metropolitan Interdenomi-
national Church in Nashville, Tennessee. A product of self-motivation, his congregation is diverse in every aspect.

A PRAYER AGAINST RACISM

Master, I know you are no respecter of person. May the partition walls that divide your sincere followers be broken down by the spirit of love. Though in a slave country, I know, Omnipresent one, that thou art with me. He that feareth God and worketh righteousness shall be accepted of him, not he who hath a different skin. Not he who belongs to this denomination, or to that, but he that feareth God.

God, you know the secrets of all hearts. Favor us with your presence, O God. Display your power by a general outpouring of the spirit. May sinners cry for mercy, while others shout for joy. May we be faithful stewards of the manifold gifts of God and never be ashamed to confess what the Lord has done for us. May we never lose the witness out of the heart by withholding our testimony from our friends and neighbors of your power to save. May we not just run well for a season, and yield to the temptation of the tempter's whisper saying "not now" and by and by the soul becomes barren and unfruitful. May we "watch" and tell around what a dear Savior we have found.

—JARENA LEE (1783–18??)

In 1817, Jarena Lee was ordained the first female minister of the African Methodist Episcopal Church by Reverend Richard Allen. She published a book, *The Life and Religious Experiences of Jarena Lee*, in 1836—one of the first autobiographical texts written by a black woman.

A PRAYER AGAINST INJUSTICE

Great God of justice, grant that the dark night of injustice will give way to the dawning of a brighter day. Give thy people respite from the heat of constant battle. But never let us give up until the victory is won. Forgive us our complacency, for we will do better, or we will die. Help us to always protest against evil. But also give us the strength to produce the good. In the Name of the Name about every name.

Amen.

—Dr. Mack King Carter

Presently serving as pastor of Mount Olive Baptist Church in Fort Lauderdale, Florida, Dr. Carter has taught at various colleges in Kentucky and has also lectured internationally. Among the highlights of his career, he has been a guest preacher in the National Baptist Convention, and in 1986 was guest speaker at a prayer breakfast in honor of the prime minister of the Bahamian government, Sir Lynden O. Pindling, in celebration of thirteen years of Bahamian independence.

PSALM 71: ASSIST OUR DEFENSE LAWYERS

O God, assist our defense lawyers;
lend thy help to our legal counsel
before the bar of southern justice.
For here the courtrooms are no longer
halls of equal justice under the law.

Give thy aid, O God;
render thy hand in favor of the oppressed.
Argue along with our attorneys
against the iniquities before us;
join in our pleas to the court.

"Your honor, we object," we constantly shout;
"we object to racism,
we object to human exploitation,
we object to judicial repression,
and we object to the violation of human rights."

O God, we pray for justice;
we scream for truth.
Come into this courtroom, O God,
and assist our defense lawyers;
give aid to attorney Ferguson and our other lawyers.

—REVEREND DR. BENJAMIN F. CHAVIS, JR.

Born in Oxford, North Carolina, in 1948, Dr. Chavis has been actively involved in the civil rights movement for more than thirty-five years. He is currently national director of the Million Man March, Inc., and is also an ordained minister of the United Church of Christ. In 1972, he was wrongly convicted of having incited race riots, and ended up spending four years in jail. Deeply rooted in his religious beliefs, yet filled with anguish at the injustice he suffered, Dr. Chavis wrote the book *Psalms from Prison*, from which this prayer was taken.

PRAYER TO ASPIRE TO JUSTICE

O God, our help in ages past, our hope for years to come, our shelter from the stormy blast, and our eternal home. To you, God, be the glory for the things Thou hast done. O Divine master, Thou Who art almighty and all powerful, loving, patient, kind, and wonderfully gracious. Thou Who constantly awaits the petitions and adoration of praise and thanksgiving from Your creatures. We thank Thee that Thou has placed in us a spark of divinity wherein our souls cannot rest until they rest in Thee. This requires us to do what is right in Thy sight. Therefore, we come restless before Your throne of grace, knowing we have been quiet when we should have spoken, and spoken when we should have remained quiet. We have been negligent in helping justice to roll down like a mighty stream.

Lord, strengthen me that I may fight wholeheartedly against racism, sexism, classism, ageism, and all other acts of oppression which demoralize both the oppressors and the oppressed. Let my fight for liberation be authentic rather than just a struggle for self-aggrandizement. Rid me of the narrowness of my mind. Help me not to have a tunnel vision, but rather to view life from the perspectives of all Your children. Give us courage now to correct the evilness of our ways, and give us strength to go forth and without bias, to investigate truth so that all may see Your kingdom realized here on earth. In Jesus' name.

Amen.

—REVEREND CHESTINA MITCHELL ARCHIBALD

Once true justice is achieved, many of the problems that create a need for restitution or punishment will disappear. "To do justice and judgment is more acceptable to the Lord than sacrifice" (Proverbs 21:3).

In the Wake of Tragedy

Lord, the psalmist asked, how long O Lord, how long will Thou hide Thyself from me. Today, God, there are terrible disasters which take the lives of many people. It is hard to recognize Your hand in such a tragedy, but I pray that through such tribulations, many people can come to a deepened relationship with You, even a new relationship with You, as we recognize the frailty of our physical existence and the lack of control we have over it. Perhaps You use these opportunities to knock at the hearts of those affected by these calamities, and I pray they let You in. No matter what tribulations arise in this life, if we have You dwelling in our hearts, we are sure to overcome. In Christ's Name.

Amen.

—Reverend Chestina Mitchell Archibald

No one welcomes tragedy, but the power of God may eventually turn turmoil into blessing. Reverend Archibald looks to Galatians 5:22 for comfort: "But the fruit of the Spirit is love, joy, peace, longsuffering, gentleness, faith."

TENEMENT FIRES

Did you hear those sirens last night, Lord?
They sound like lamentations.
You can hear the cry come unto you.
"Save the children . . . save the children . . ."
Seven of the children died in the fire on Whiton Street.
All huddled up against the windows.
Dead.
A lot of people die
    in the fires of slums and tenements in the city.
A lot of people lose
    what little furniture and clothing they own.
When you live in the firetraps of the city,
there is never any insurance.

Lord, the fire kept burning up the stairs . . .
    Up the stairs, Lord!
There wasn't any fire escape
    and the stairs, Lord, just weren't there any more.
They were so scared, Lord,
    so scared they couldn't move anymore—
seven children and their mother.
All that smoke—
    they couldn't breathe.
The landlord and the city inspector
    had choked off the air long ago.
Lord, you know that's no way to live and die—with no air
    to breathe.
Going to bed at night
    not knowing if you will be alive in the morning.

All that crummy wiring and those kerosene stoves.
Once it starts, that's it, Lord.
So, Lord, this prayer
    is about helping the people to organize in these firetraps
    not to pay any rent
    until the owner and city get with it.
Help us to sleep safe tonight—
    the sirens still,
    the children in your ever-loving arms.
Suffer the little children, Lord.
    Amen.

—ROBERT W. CASTLE, JR.

In addition to *Prayers from the Burned-Out City* (1968), Robert W. Castle, Jr., has also contributed his writing to other books, including *On the Battle Lines, The Underground Church,* and *II Living Room Dialogues.* An Episcopal priest, he has ministered at numerous religious institutions. *Prayers from the Burned-Out City* is a collection of prayers "born out of poverty and war" that were written to give strength to those living in urban areas and to uplift the faith of those who may be filled with bitterness and anger because of their current circumstances.

A PRAYER OF THANKS AND CONSOLATION

Eternal God, our Father in Heaven, we thank You for Your love, Your kindness, and for the "peace which passeth all understanding." We give You thanks for Your Son, Jesus Christ, who has provided us with power, faith, healing, and the Holy Spirit, who helps us to hold out during these troubled times.

According to Your word in Matthew 7:7, You said, "Ask and it shall be given unto us, seek and we can find, knock and it will be opened unto us." Jesus, we believe what You said, so we are asking, we are seeking and knocking. We believe as a people that You will save us as a people. You will forgive us from our mistakes and heal us from our sins.

Some of our homes and some of our youth have been shattered by mistrust and doubt about the future. Our faith has been dismantled by disparity. Lord, we need You to comfort us with Your comforting spirit. Lift us up to where we belong. Give us that light that shines only from Your presence. Provide us with that faith that will not shrink. We ask this, in the name of Jesus.

    Amen.

—REVEREND DONALD ADKINS

Reverend Adkins is a husband and the father of six children, among them actor-comedian Sinbad. He has been pastor of Second Baptist Church in Benton Harbor, Michigan, for more than thirty years. Among his many notable achievements, he organized the Berrien OIC, a national training program for the disadvantaged and unemployed, and he continues to serve the organization as chairman of the board. In July 1992, he was honored by the mayor of Benton Harbor in the naming of Donald Adkins Drive, the street on which Second Baptist Church is located. He is active in many community organizations and is affiliated with the Chain Lake District Organization, the NAACP, the National Baptist Convention, and the Wolverine State Convention.

A Prayer for Peace

Sovereign Lord, creator of Life Glory, Dominion, and Praise to Your Holy name.

Lord, in the midst of conflict, in the presence of threat of harm by ungodly men, and during times of rampant terrorism, we pray that your perfect will be performed in the earth.

As soldiers for our country, we prepare and execute our duties. Keep us during these times. Give us fighting strength, for we learn that often peace can only come by fighting. Use us, dear Lord, as vessels of peace for our country and our world.

In times of fear and distress, instill a spirit of peace within us, that we may carry out our mission.

In the spirit of thanksgiving for this peace and in the name of Christ the glorified One we pray.

Amen.

—Reverend Darren White

A resident of Nashville, Tennessee, Reverend White is currently serving at Faith, Hope and Love Fellowship. He has also been a captain in the United States Army Reserve Corps.

A PRAYER AGAINST WAR

Almighty God,

To me war seems like such a terrible reality. My hope is that my children will not have to endure war, and my heart goes out to all who must suffer it. In the Old Testament, there are numerous wars recorded which seem to have been necessary for Your people to prevail. Oh, my glorious God, surely some wars are not necessary for Your will on earth, surely some are a manifestation of selfishness, greed, and desire for power. Please inspire the minds of the leaders of Nations to unite and live peacefully. If there are wars, I pray for those close to Your heart to be the victors and for them to bestow Your graciousness on those who they conquer, displaying divine forgiveness and love. Through war, let greater peace prevail. Please guide us in time of war and peace. God, and give us strength.

    Amen.

—REVEREND CHESTINA MITCHELL ARCHIBALD

The Old Testament prophets foresaw a day when peace would reign on earth. We should express our faith by putting forth the effort to make that day come in our lifetimes. "And he shall judge among the nations, and shall rebuke many people: and they shall beat their swords into ploughshares, and their spears into pruning hooks: nation shall not lift up sword against nation, neither shall they learn war any more" (Isaiah 2:4).

A Prayer for Peace

My Father God and my Mother God, I come to thee asking that you would be kind enough to answer this prayer and grant my humble request at this time. You are the only God who has answered the prayers of your people for generations past and generations to come. Great God, hear now my plea for peace in this city. Hear now my plea for peace in our homes and families. Hear now my plea for peace in our world. I believe that you are listening and that you will honor this request. I thank you now by faith. In Jesus's name.

    Amen.

—Reverend H. Carlyle Church, Jr.

Reverend Church is a graduate of The American University in Washington, D.C. He is currently serving as a member of the Ph.D. Task Force at the Howard University School of Divinity, also located in Washington, D.C., where he received his master of divinity degree.

PEACE IN THE COMMUNITY

O God, we stretch our hands to Thee for no other help we know, if Thou withdraw Thyself from us, O wither shall we go?

We come with our hearts heavily burdened. For when we look around, there is trouble on every hand. Some children are either selling or using drugs. Consequently, our neighborhoods are not safe. There are drive-by shootings, burglaries, car jackings, and all types of violent crimes. We are calling on You, O God, because we know that You love us too much to forsake us and are too true to Your word not to be with us in our time of need. You promised never to leave us alone! So we are asking You to do something to give us the assurance that You are with us during our turmoil. Do something! Do something, O God, to help us to be better parents, better neighbors, and better citizens. That we may be able to realize that we are our brother's and sister's keeper. And we will be very careful to give You all the praise, all the glory, and all the honor—all we want is the blessing of being able to live in a peaceful community. Amen! Amen!

—REVEREND OTIS L. WELDON, SR.

Reverend Weldon, of Lithonia, Georgia, says of his prayer: "It gives me hope and reassurance that in spite of all the problems and trouble in our community, God is still with us." We are reminded that it is the duty of each one of us, as God's children, to work hard to make our community one that reflects God's will.

A Prayer Against Crime

Dear God,

This world is riddled with violence and hatred. I pray for the hearts and souls of humankind to be freed from the bondage of hatred, blessed with peace, and filled with the bounty of Your love. I pray in repentance on behalf of those who have acted violently against others. Open all of our minds to be receptive to the unction of the Holy Spirit that makes all things plain. Help us to discern the difference between individual and corporate sins. Both often lead to crime. Enable us to do more than merely observe these problems in the world, but give us the courage of Harriet Tubman, Sojourner Truth, or Ida B. Wells, that we may dare to fight to make this a better world.

Amen.

—Reverend Chestina Mitchell Archibald

If we sit back and observe the wrongs of the world without trying to help, we may be as guilty as those who actually commit crimes. We must set an example through right action, as well as speaking out against the wrongs that we see. "But let none of you suffer as a murderer, or as a thief, or as an evil doer, or as a busybody . . ." (1 Peter 4:15).

AGAINST CHURCH DESECRATION

Lord, there are many sinister acts happening here. Persons seek to destroy the very edifices that symbolize belief in Thee. I don't agree with these acts, Lord, but I think I understand them. Anyone who has witnessed the strength of Your ebony children, and the continuous upward move in spite of every roadblock, must know that it comes from a power that is not our own. Like Delilah, who sought to know the source of Samson's strength, the inquiry continues: What makes them so strong?

Lord, help those who feel so insecure that they fear the progress of others. May they find You and be healed. In Jesus's name, I pray,
Amen.

—REVEREND CHESTINA MITCHELL ARCHIBALD

Sometimes what feels like weakness may actually be proof of our strength. Outsiders attack what they do not understand, fearing it because they sense an invincible source of strength. "But none of these things move me, neither count I my life dear unto myself, so that I might finish my course with joy, and the ministry, which I have received of the Lord Jesus, to testify the gospel of the grace of God" (Acts 20:24).

AGAINST DOMESTIC VIOLENCE

Lord, many are in destructive marriages, yet wish to state, as Your Word suggests: "Til death do us part." Thank you, Lord, for granting us the spiritual discernment to know that You did not mean only the death of one's body, but also the death of one's spirit, and even the death of the contract. As Nicodemus came to know, one does not have to re-enter his mother's womb to be born again, and neither does one have to die a physical death to be dead.

Give those who are being abused the strength needed to stand up to the abuser or give them the courage to leave. Grant the abusers Your grace and mercy. Draw them closer to You, that persons may find spiritual nourishment for empty souls. In Christ's name, we pray,
Amen.

—REVEREND CHESTINA MITCHELL ARCHIBALD

When two people marry, they become one in spirit. Therefore, when we hurt our partner, we hurt ourselves. We must seek God's grace for our partner as well as ourselves. "Entreat me not to leave thee . . . thy people shall be my people, and thy God my God" (Ruth 1:16).

AGAINST VICTIMIZATION

Many fall victim to satan's trickery. Rescue them quickly and revive them. Help all to be wise and cautious to avoid pitfalls. Empowered by Your word and love, we can stand strong against any attack on our spirits.

Many have suffered abuse and have had evil afflicted on them or their loved ones. It is an emotional roller-coaster ride for anyone who is a victim of ill-treatment, notwithstanding one's level of faith. It is easy to lose sight of who you are when one's physical self is constantly endangered. I pray we can all be strengthened by Your spirit and thus become sensitive to our surroundings so we can avoid becoming victims. But, if ever victimized, Lord, please give us the strength of heart to do all in our power to protect ourselves, then be able to forgive the abuser and continue to love ourselves.

Finally, Lord, let me not be a victim of any circumstances, but allow me to be the ruler of my destiny, centered on Your will. In Christ's Name,

Amen.

—REVEREND CHESTINA MITCHELL ARCHIBALD

We must pray for strength to resist physical pain and overcome emotional hurt, acknowledging that, just as a force outside of ourselves can cause hurt, a greater power beyond ourselves can help us to heal. "Fret not thyself because of evildoers . . . they shall soon be cut down like the grass, and wither as the green herb" (Psalms 37:1–2).

A PRAYER FOR WHEN A LOVED ONE PASSES AWAY

O Gracious and Almighty God, You who knoweth from whence we have come and where we are going, even though we do not know these things about ourselves. We come at this moment of difficulty to submit our way to Your divine will. Lord, You have said in Your word: If we ask, it shall be given; if we seek, we shall find; if we knock, doors shall be opened to us. We come to You now asking that You give us the strength to release our loved one back to You in a spirit of gratitude, knowing that there will be no more suffering, no more heartaches, no more disappointments. Help us to rejoice that there is rest from all labor, that there is peace that passes all understanding, and that there is unspeakable joy when union is formed with that caravan of innumerable ancestors that have gone on before and is able, with all the host of heaven, to welcome one more new member.

Lord, we seek greater faith. Remove all doubt. Help our unbelief. And now as our beloved stands knocking at the door of eternal life, may we be reminded of our own immortality that we may immediately rise from our slumber of pity and be about the unfinished business that is before us. Teach us to forgive, forget, and to love, so that the remainder of our journey may be pleasing in Your sight. As we commend this spirit into Your hands, give us life anew that we, like our Savior, will be able, in all things, to pray not our will but Thine. In Thy Holy name, we pray.

Amen.

—REVEREND CHESTINA MITCHELL ARCHIBALD

Death is not the end of our relationship with God; rather, it marks a fresh start, with new insight into God's being. This applies to our relationships with others as well. "Be thou faithful unto death, and I will give thee a crown of life." (Revelation 2:10).

THE DREADED EXTINGUISHER OF LIFE

We weep today because we do not understand why the dreaded extinguisher, death, visits our communities and takes away our sons, fathers, husbands, uncles, nephews. Some were so young, healthy and strong, and yet they are gone.

Lord Jesus, it is hard for us to see death the way you saw it, as a gateway to a greater life. That is why we mourn.

Help us to understand the concept, that in the midst of life we are in death. We know it is inevitable, but still we mourn.

It is so painful when a loved one dies, and we ask you to comfort us and we thank you, Lord, for being there all night long and all day long when we need a shoulder to cry on.

We know that one day you will explain this unwanted guest, death, to us, but right now we ask you to grant us inner peace, though there is no outward joy, as we mourn those so near and dear to us.

—PASTOR JAMES L. DAVIS

Commenting on the theme of his prayer, Pastor Davis, of the Big Bethel African Methodist Episcopal Church in Atlanta, Georgia, says: "Death is the dreaded extinguisher because we enjoy life and we do not understand death. This prayer was inspired by the recent execution-style killing of four black adult males in Atlanta, and the death of one teenager in an unrelated gang killing in March 1996."

A Prayer on the Value of Tradition

Great God of the Universe,
Here in America, we have a great variety of people from different racial and cultural backgrounds. All have their various traditions, yet, many have lost sight of the value of these traditions.

Please help me to recognize and promote significant traditions that strengthen society and uphold moral principles. Inspire Your people to value such traditions and take the time to embody them. Let heavenly traditions reign forever. Help us to pioneer great new traditions for those who follow You. Bring us closer as a people united in Christ's name. Let us not waste precious time with useless traditions. Help us break away from traditions which separate people or do not include You. I pray for the heavenly tradition to arise that includes all humankind. Inspire us to seek out and follow Your tradition, based on Jesus' words and lifestyle. I know we can fulfill Your ultimate plan if we open our hearts and truly offer our lives to You. Then our future will not be thwarted by tragic traps of the past, but we will instead be able to see a new heaven and a new earth, where all dare remain different from the other, but placed beside each other make up Your Rainbow of Hope. In Christ's Name.
    Amen.

—Reverend Chestina Mitchell Archibald

Rituals are sacred when they contain basic truths that glorify God; rituals become insignificant when their inspiration fails to touch the divine. "[I]n vain do they worship . . . for laying aside the commandment of God, ye hold the tradition of men" (Mark 7:7–8).

A PRAYER ON THE SIGNIFICANCE OF ART

God, we come remembering that yesterday influences today's condition. Our remembering of those past experiences which have survived in names, stones, stories, steel, wood and film is the gathering of the icons of our individual and collective humanity that provides the sustenance for a more sane tomorrow.

—PROFESSOR EARL J. HOOKS

Internationally known for his artistic ability, Earl Hooks is professor emeritus of art at Fisk University in Nashville, Tennessee. His work as an artist explores many different dimensions and perspectives of life.

My Last Will and Testament

If I have a legacy to leave my people, it is my philosophy of living and serving. Here, then, is My Legacy . . . I leave you hope. Yesterday, our ancestors endured the degradation of slavery, yet they retained their dignity. I leave you the challenge of developing confidence in one another. This kind of confidence will aid the economic rise of the race by bringing together the pennies and dollars of our people and ploughing them into useful channels.

I leave you thirst for education. Knowing is the prime need of our hours.

I leave you respect for the uses of power. Power, intelligently directed, can lead to more freedom.

I leave you faith. Faith in God is the greatest power, but great, too, is faith in oneself.

I leave you racial dignity. I want Negroes to maintain their human dignity at all costs.

I leave you a desire to live harmoniously with your fellow man.

—MARY MCLEOD BETHUNE (1875–1955)

Mary McLeod Bethune, the daughter of South Carolina sharecroppers, went on to become adviser to the president of the United States, and was the American delegate to the first United Nations conference. A woman who surpassed all odds, she left behind a great contribution to society in the form of an educational institution: Bethune College (which, after later merging with Cookman College, is known today as Bethune-Cookman College).

A PRAYER ON SELF-ESTEEM

Lord, You have made me pecan tan, a sort of honey-hush brown. I glisten in the sun's rays, and mellow in the moon's light. You've given me a natural tan, and for this beauty I am most grateful.

But, Lord, I am also grateful for my inner beauty of love and peace, of happiness that ignites like fire, and in my presence others get a glimpse of Your glory and affirm Your presence in me.

Thank you, God, for making me who I am, wonderfully beautiful in body, mind, and spirit.

Amen.

—REVEREND CHESTINA MITCHELL ARCHIBALD

Believing in ourselves, and appreciating all that God has offered us by giving us life, is an expression of belief in God. Confidence in ourselves reflects confidence in the God who created us. "Judge me, O Lord, for I have walked in mine integrity . . . that I publish with the voice of thanksgiving, and tell of all thy wondrous works and he that hath it shall abide satisfied" (Psalms 26:1, 7); "The fear of the Lord leads to life; and he who has it rests satisfied; he will not be visited by harm" (Proverbs 19:23).

A PRAYER ON UNITY

I pray for unity of all people. There are so many conflicting religions and cultures and ideas. Help us to find common ground by seeing the image of You in each other. Inspire us to look beyond the differences which divide us. Let us not bicker over trivial matters, but inspire us to practice Jesus's love and service. Let each of us attempt to embody Christ and live as He did. Open our selfish eyes and help us put aside petty grievances. God, You are the alpha and the omega—I pray for Your will to come quickly on earth, as in Heaven. Amen.

—REVEREND CHESTINA MITCHELL ARCHIBALD

Regardless of where we were born and what belief system we follow, we are all brothers and sisters in the eyes of our loving divine parent. We must all work together to create a spirit of love and acceptance within our universal family. "Behold, how good and how pleasant it is for brethren to dwell together in unity!" (Psalms 133:1).

CELEBRATING OUR ONENESS AS A FAMILY OF HUMANKIND

Creator and Sustainer of all humankind:

Thank you for giving us the marvelous opportunity of working with persons of all races and of many nations. As we have lived in various homes, worshiped in various churches, and taught in many schools, we have felt in the depths of our being the reality—now—of the family of humankind.

You, the Creator, are one. You have made each one of us, so we are all brothers and sisters. Forgive us for focusing on our differences of race, ethnicity, and religious heritage. Help us to celebrate the wonderful diversity of your creation—of plants and animals and persons—rather than feel threatened by it. Remind us once again that love holds all things together.

Fill us with your Spirit and with the mind of Christ, so that we see clearly the world's evil but put our trust in the triumph of goodness and love. As Easter people, strengthen us to work for one world of brothers and sisters, pulled together by love and worship of you, Creator and Sustainer of all humankind. We pray in the name of our Redeemer, Jesus Christ, the daily companion of our way.

    Amen.

—DR. FRED CLOUD

Currently president of Human Relations Consultation Services in Nashville, Tennessee, Dr. Cloud is also professor of sociology and psychology at American Baptist College and editor-in-chief of the *Journal of Intergroup Relations.* In addition, he has also contributed considerably to the betterment of human rights, acting as president of the National Association of Human Rights Workers (1972–1973) and as vice president of the International Association of Official Human Rights Agencies (1971–1973).

ETHNICITY

Dear Creator of Us All,

We are blessed to be precious flowers in your garden. We are different colors, different sizes, different shapes, different aromas, but we all have a distinct and holy purpose.

Reign on us and in us that by faith we may stand in beauty, whole and complete in your presence. Teach us that our true nourishment is in the grace and mercy of your Son.

In Him we pray,
    Amen.

—MICHAEL PURYEAR

Michael Puryear is a songwriter from Nashville, Tennessee. In his prayer, we are reminded that God's glory is reflected in each of us, and that we should celebrate our differences in race, gender, nationality, religion, age, or appearance.

Prayers for Different Members of the Community

Now therefore, I pray Thee, if I have found grace in Thy sight, show me now Thy way, that I may know Thee, that I may find grace in Thy sight.

EXODUS 33:13

A Prayer for Men

Lord God, who art perfect and who has sent Jesus as a perfect example of what it means to be fully human and fully Divine, I come now in my humanness seeking to get more in touch with the Divine. Help me to see both the strength and the vulnerability; the boldness and the humility; the rebuking and the redeeming natures of Jesus. Help me to recognize in Jesus what it truly means to be a man of God. I surrender and place myself anew in Your hands, and like clay in the potter's hands, I ask that You mold me after Your will, "while I am waiting yielded and still." In the name of Jesus, I pray.

Amen.

—Reverend Chestina Mitchell Archibald

Because God sent His Son as the perfect example of what a man should be, one must pray to God for the strength and courage to model their ways after Jesus's. As it is written in Mark 16:16a: "He that believeth and is baptized shall be saved . . ."

A Prayer for Women

Dear God, Mother of All Creation,
Grant all women a deep, abiding understanding of Your purpose for their lives. You have made women strong, yet loving, decisive leaders, yet nurturers; you have made women in Your divine image. For this, Lord, we are most grateful. Please now grant women the fortitude to burst loose. Help them to throw off any shackle that might be holding them in bondage. As Your divine helpers, shield them from fear as they realize that You are with them even unto the ends of the earth.

    Amen.

—Reverend Chestina Mitchell Archibald

Illustrated in this prayer is the unique and special purpose that God reserved for women. Women must look to God for the courage to stand strong while simultaneously maintaining their nurturing qualities. Inspiration for this prayer came from Isaiah 50:9a: "Behold the Lord God will help me; who is he that shall condemn me?"

A Prayer for Writers

O God of All Creation,
It is said that the pen is mightier than the sword. O God, please use this pen to write great words for Your sake. Please speak through my writings to awaken others to Your existence and will. One's ideas receive a degree of immortality through books—let these ideas be worthy of preservation. The Bible is inspired writing that is valuable for all time. I pray You can use me and others as vessels to write Your words that will give hope, strengthen faith, and open all to Your love. In Christ's Name.

    Amen.

—Reverend Chestina Mitchell Archibald

The highly inspirational and motivational writings in the Bible are the most cherished words ever written—we are blessed to have inherited its legacy. We pray to God to speak through us, so that the writings we might produce can spread His glorious word and uplift lives. In the writing of this prayer, Reverend Archibald was influenced by Exodus 17:14a: "And the Lord said . . . Write this for a memorial in a book, and rehearse it in the ears . . ."

INVOCATION

Oh Lord of Hosts, my thoughts inspire,
My mind with lofty ideals fire,
My song attune, my theme direct,
Guide thou my word, my words select,
Thy wisdom give, thy grace impart,
Let inspiration fill my heart;
My helpless self in thy arms hold,
While I this tale of woe unfold.

On my weak effort shed thy light,
Courage impart, remove all fright;
Let latent powers within me wake,
Proneness to error from me take.
My tongue endow with proper speech,
Increase my wisdom I beseech;
Me deluge with the needful aid,
Uphold me lest I be dismayed.

—MAURICE N. CORBETT (1859–192?)

Born in Yanceyville, North Carolina, Maurice Corbett was educated at Shaw University. He served in the North Carolina Legislature and was a delegate to numerous political conventions. In 1919, he was stricken with paralysis. This prayer is taken from *The Harp of Ethiopia,* an epic poem in which Corbett chronicles the entire history of blacks in America.

A Prayer on Traveling

I pray that in all my travels, Lord, You will make yourself known, that I may see You in all places and also be a vessel for You to work through that others may see You. I always appreciate this sacred quiet time that we have to spend together. Even though I have to drive, at least I am away from the phone, the television, and other blatant interruptions. As I travel, I stop along the way to savor Your wonderful creations of nature—often it is at these moments when I feel most close to You. I know You are guiding and protecting me as a shepherd does his sheep. Thanks for precious time and safe travel.

Amen.

—Reverend Chestina Mitchell Archibald

Reverend Archibald was inspired by Isaiah 63:1 in the writing of this prayer: "Who is this that cometh . . . travelling in the greatness of his strength? . . . mighty to save." When we make a journey, we can feel secure in the knowledge that God is watching over us, protecting us, and leading us on our way as we rejoice in the glory of His land.

FOR SAINTS IN OUR MIDST

God,

I offer up this prayer to ask for Your protection and blessing to be bestowed upon the saints of this world. You know who they are and You know well their tribulations. Please uplift their spirits so that they can continue to bring blessings into the world through their selfless acts centered on You. May the saints of the world rise up with new power and glory and lead the way to Your kingdom.

Amen.

—REVEREND CHESTINA MITCHELL ARCHIBALD

There are those among us who transcend what is typical of human nature and devote themselves to the glorification of God, incorporating His will into all their deeds. We pray that these exceptional persons are able to bestow upon the world the manifestation of God's will, and are always protected by Him. The inspiration for this prayer was found in 2 Corinthians 9:8: "And God is able to make all grace abound toward you; that ye, always having all sufficiency in all things, may abound to every good work."

PRAYER FOR THOSE CONSIDERING
THE MINISTRY

Lord, it is You who formed me in my mother's womb and shut within my bones the blazing fire of Your Holy Spirit. I have done all in my power to quench its flame, but ne'er can I run from its presence.

Like Abraham and Sarah, I sometimes think I'm too old; like Jeremiah, I sometimes think I'm too young; like Moses, I feel inadequate for the task as I sometimes feel incapable of speaking on Your behalf. Like Peter, I sometimes feel like no more than a drunken sailor; like Paul, I sometimes feel there is a thorn in my flesh. Yet I know that in Your infinite wisdom You still see fit to call me.

Lord, I have prayed, I have meditated, I have wept, I have mourned. I have run to the mountains; like Jonah, I have gone to the sea; but like all of Your prophets of old, I find there is no hiding place. So now, Lord, like your darling son Jesus, who asked You to take away the bitter cup, but then surrendered and said, *Not My will but Thine*, into Thine hand I commend my spirit. Lord, in the words of Isaiah: "Here I am, Lord, send me." I'll go where You say to go; I'll do what You say to do; I'll be what You say for me to be. Lord, I humbly repent for having run so long. I now come wholly to Thee through the blood and precious name of Jesus Christ, I pray.

Amen.

—REVEREND CHESTINA MITCHELL ARCHIBALD

In the writing of this prayer, Reverend Archibald was motivated by 2 Peter 1:11: "For so an entrance shall be ministered unto you abundantly into the everlasting Kingdom of our Lord and Saviour Jesus Christ." The prayer illustrates how those who are called by God to the ministry cannot ignore the presence of the Holy Spirit in their souls and must respond to this divine challenge with humble gratitude and a sincere heart.

A Pastoral Prayer

O God, our Heavenly Father, we thank thee for this golden privilege to worship thee, the only true God of the universe. We come to thee today, grateful that thou hast kept us through the long night of the past and ushered us into the challenge of the present and the bright hope of the future. We are mindful, O God, that man cannot save himself, for man is not the measure of things and humanity is not God. Bound by our chains of sins and finiteness, we know we need a Savior. We thank thee, O God, for the spiritual nature of man. We are in nature but we live above nature. Help us never to let anybody or any condition pull us so low as to cause us to hate. Give us strength to love our enemies and to do good to those who despitefully use us and persecute us. We thank thee for thy Church, founded upon thy Word, that challenges us to do more than sing and pray, but go out and work as though the very answer to our prayers depended on us and not upon thee. Then, finally, help us to realize that man was created to shine like stars and live on through all eternity. Keep us, we pray, in perfect peace; help us to walk together, pray together, sing together, and live together until that day when all God's children, Black, White, Red, and Yellow will rejoice in one common band of humanity in the kingdom of our Lord and of our God, we pray.

Amen.

—Martin Luther King, Jr.

One of the world's best-known advocates of nonviolent social change, Martin Luther King, Jr., produced ideas based on various traditions and practices from cultures around the world. The son and grandson of ministers in the African American Baptist church, King later went on to become a Baptist minister himself. Among his most notable accomplishments, in 1957 he founded the Southern

Christian Leadership Conference (SCLC), which emphasized the goal of voting rights for blacks. In addition, he organized numerous marches—the most famous at which he delivered his celebrated "I Have a Dream" speech to 250,000 people in Washington, D.C. (August 28, 1963). He received the Nobel Peace Prize for his work in December 1964, and he will always be remembered for his exceptional contributions to all races.

A Prayer for Ministers

All-loving, all-caring God, provider of all our needs, we say thanks. Thank You for doing the impossible in our lives; thank You for healing our sicknesses; thank You for your guidance; and thank You for ministering to us in our every hour of need. We now ask that You use us in ministry to others. We know that we live in a world full of pain and sorrow. Help us to be comforters and edifiers. Lord, help us to walk as Jesus did in ministry to all the world. And Lord, help us to do ministry not according to our selfish plans, but Your divine and loving will. In the name of Jesus, the minister to all the world, we pray.

Amen.

—Reverend Chestina Mitchell Archibald

As it is said in Mark 16:15: "Go ye into all the world, and preach the gospel to every creature." God needs His earthly clergy to go forth and spread His word throughout the world, serving as examples of His divine goodness.

BLESSINGS OF THE MINISTRY

Lord, grant us health as we labor under difficulty. Bless our labors abundantly so our hearts can rejoice to witness the outpouring of the Holy Spirit. Help our preaching to move beyond denominations, and give us liberty in speaking. We place ourselves in Your hands and stay there as clay in the hands of the potter. Give us liberty, whereby we can hear the humble groans of the people. We bless you, Lord that the Gospel has never been left without a witness.

Thank You, Lord, for the fulfillment of Your word. As Joel prophesied, "Ye shall know that I am in the midst of Israel, and that I am the Lord, your God, and none else, and My people shall never be ashamed. And it shall come to pass afterwards, that I will pour out My spirit upon your flesh, and your sons and your daughters shall prosper."

You promised that our old men shall dream dreams, and that our young men shall see visions. Cause our eye of faith to see people march like armies. Thanks for assuring us of comfort as we wait upon the Lord.

Amen.

—REVEREND CHESTINA MITCHELL ARCHIBALD

This prayer describes the desires of those chosen by God to enter the ministry to have the strength, wisdom, and power to help heal the poor in spirit and to remain messengers of His holy word on earth. God's promise to those who have devoted themselves to the church is confirmed in Deuteronomy 15:18: "And the Lord thy God shall bless thee in all that thou doest."

FOR THE MINISTRY

Heavenly Father,

I pray continually for the saints at our church and for our TV audience. I pray that as they hear the Word, they will be doers of Your Word and not just hearers only. That they will continue to desire the sincere milk of the Word that they may grow in grace and in the knowledge of Jesus Christ. That they may have the Spirit of wisdom and revelation knowledge of Your will and of Your Word, that the eyes of their understanding will be enlightened daily, and that they may make right decisions in their lives so that they may be blameless in Your presence. I pray that they walk in the Spirit and that they shall not fulfill the lusts of the flesh, that they live holy lives, that they walk in divine health, divine prosperity and that all their needs are met according to your riches in glory by Christ Jesus. I pray for the workers at our church, that they will do their work as unto You out of a motive of love, knowing that You will reward them.

Now Father, I commit this day to You that all that I do this day may be done to the praise and glory and honor of Your name. In Jesus' Name I pray.

I pray for employees and I thank You for them and pray that they will do their work as unto You out of a motive of love knowing that You will reward them. Thank you continually for exposing, revealing, or removing anyone or anything in order that they may be placed according to Your divine will.

Amen.

—DR. FREDERICK K. C. PRICE AND DR. BETTY R. PRICE

Dr. Fred Price is founder and pastor of Crenshaw Christian Center, a seventeen thousand–member church in Los Angeles, California. His wife, Dr. Betty Price, is first lady of Crenshaw Christian Center and founder of the church's Women's Fellowship. Crenshaw Christian Center is the home of the world-renowned Faith Dome, from which the *Ever Increasing Faith* television program is broadcast weekly to one hundred twenty stations.

FOR BISHOPS

God knows bishops need our prayers.
Real prayers.
It must be hard to be so important:
     to be a bishop—one of your most chosen ones, Lord.
So much responsibility, power, position;
concern is a real burden, Lord.
Now, Lord,
when men get so much responsibility and position, they sometimes
    get scared.
A bishop shouldn't be scared, Lord.
He should be powerful and fearless in love and truth.
So, Lord,
help all bishops not to be mealy-mouths,
or too timid and afraid to live and die for truth, freedom and love.
How come,
when so many people are sitting in jail and suffering for love
and justice for all men,
so many bishops are sitting in cathedral offices?
Lord,
get all bishops out in the streets where the people are—
your people, Lord.

Help them to walk among us and to be one with us.
I think they would like to.
Lord, help them not to be afraid.
Help them to know we love them
and need them and want them.
Now!
    Amen.

—ROBERT W. CASTLE, JR.

During the course of his career, Robert W. Castle, Jr., worked as a chaplain to Protestant students at Montclair State College, in Upper Montclair, New Jersey. This excerpt from his book, *Prayers from the Burned-Out City,* is dedicated to bishops everywhere; we are made to realize that although bishops may have an important position, they have problems and quirks just like us, and we ask God to give them the strength and courage to become leaders we can look up to.

A PRAYER FOR TEACHERS

Almighty God,

Since the birth of my children, I've begun to worry about their future. Please excuse me, for You hold their futures in Your hand. Yet, I know wherever they are, You shall be there. I pray now for teachers in all schools. Intervene in these institutions. Go into each school with each teacher and every student. Make Your presence felt by children through those who guide and teach them. I pray that all teachers will realize that You are indeed alive and desiring to be a part of their classrooms. I pray that people of high moral character and God-centered consciousness will choose teaching as a profession. Please help us raise up great teachers who will radiate Your love and truth.

Amen.

—REVEREND CHESTINA MITCHELL ARCHIBALD

Reverend Archibald cites Isaiah 30:20 as her inspiration in writing this prayer: "Yet shall not thy teachers be removed into a corner any more, but thine eyes shall see thy teachers." Those who teach our youth have an enormous responsibility to influence children in a positive way, and we pray that God will speak through each teacher and help him or her to encourage students to develop high morals and honest values and to live according to God's will.

A Prayer on Teaching

O Master Teacher,

From our birth we are learning—but who is teaching us? Our parents, our environment, our neighbors, then teachers hired by schools. We are taught many rudimentary skills, and also ethics and morals by parents and/or church. What good does it do for a parent to teach a child that it is not good to smoke when the parent smokes? What good does it do for a minister to preach from the Bible and then break a commandment from You? Father, please help us to live consistently with what we teach. Please help people to see that their actions speak louder than words, and that the lessons learned from events experienced are greater than those learned from a speech. We can all be teachers if we embody Your Word.

Lord, where we look determines what we see, who we listen to determines what we hear, what we read shapes what we understand to be true. O Master, help us to see You in all things as we hear Your voice emanating from Your written word, so that what we absorb will be a lesson worth learning. In Christ's Name.

Amen.

—Reverend Chestina Mitchell Archibald

As stated in John 14:26: "[T]he Holy Ghost . . . shall teach you all things. . . ." Those who play an integral part in the influencing of children must look to God for the strength to set a fine example for youth to follow, demonstrating God's will through not only their words but also their actions.

A PRAYER FOR STUDENTS

O Lord God, we ask as the days unfold, many issues lifted and discussed, much planning made, and done, toil of mind, and wholeness of strength make known to our university community who Thou art and how Thou has reliably performed in and through Jesus Christ for the redemption of all life. It is by the grace of the Christ event we pray.

Amen.

—JAMES LAWSON

A native of Ohio, James Lawson was referred to by Martin Luther King, Jr., as "the theoretician of the non-violent movement." He has been active in the civil rights movement, and among his notable achievements he was a board member of the Southern Christian Leadership Conference and received awards from the NAACP in 1965 and 1974. His career has encompassed work as both a pastor and an educator.

A Prayer for Those in School

Lord, I have many things to study and my time seems so limited. Classes seem so difficult and doing my assignments has become burdensome. I pray for calmness and a clear mind to organize my studies and remember the many lessons I must retain. Please give me a steady heart to never give up, even when it seems insurmountable. Help me remember You are always with me. Lord, please calm me at exam time and help my thoughts flow freely so I can do my best. All I gain or accomplish I will offer to You. You alone deserve the praise and glory.

As I look around me I see people running to and fro, seeking happiness that eludes them time and again. As people get older and have many bad experiences, their hearts often close, and it is hard for You to reach them. Young people are so fresh and ready to learn, eager to please and achieve. I want to pray for students to have the strength of character to be able to see through temptations and overcome them. If youth can channel their energies toward fulfilling their ultimate life's purpose, to become spiritually, emotionally, intellectually, and physically mature, they can harness true happiness and a deep relationship with You. I pray for Your heavenly love to embrace the youth of the world. Please help them to inherently feel their divine value and to seek their full potential as Your children. I pray for them to be able to avoid pitfalls and painful life experiences, and to remain pure and open-hearted. Please guide and protect each so that they may work hard and become great doers of Your will. In Christ's Name.

Amen.

—Reverend Chestina Mitchell Archibald

God's desire for education of all people is found in Matthew 28:19a, 20a: "Go ye therefore, and teach all nations . . . teaching them to observe all things . . ." From an early age, young people must be taught values and morals based on God's will; from this they will learn to develop a strong character, able to turn their backs firmly on evil and to direct their eyes and hearts toward God for guidance.

A STUDENT PRAYER

O God,

Bless me with a community that understands me,
Supports me,
Loves me,
Prays for me.
With a place to return
When I reach the depths of my existence
And when I experience joy only You could send me.
Bless me with people
In whose eyes I might look
To see myself.

And . . .

Bless me with people
Who might sometimes be perplexed by my existence,
With people I might sometimes find it hard to accept,
So that we can learn from one another's differences.
Show Yourself to me
In ways that will
Broaden my understanding of You.
And most of all,
Bless me with a place
Where nothing
And no one
Interferes with Your will for me.

—MENDI D. S. LEWIS

Mendi Lewis is a recent graduate of Spelman College in Atlanta, Georgia, who is currently studying Spanish in Chapel Hill, North Carolina, at Duke University. Raised by parents who emphasized the values of education, she has come to greatly appreciate the gifts of knowledge and wisdom that God has given.

LET MY MAJOR REFLECT MY MASTER
A Prayer for Students

———

Lord, as I pursue my degree let me not forget Thee. May everything I do be reflective of You: Help me to do well in Biology, but let me not neglect You as the Rose of Sharon and the Lily of the Valleys. Let me excel in Astronomy, but let me keep my eye on the Bright and Morning Star! I want to make *A*s in Science and Pre-Med, but I must not forget that You are the Doctor of all; one who has more medicine in the hem of Your garment than in all the pharmaceutical companies of the world. Let me rise to the top in Business and Marketing, but still stay close to You who were shrewd enough to pay Your taxes from a fish's mouth. You even threatened to put the restaurants, hospitals, and funeral homes out of business through feeding the five thousand, healing the sick and raising the dead! Yes, and I do want to succeed in Agriculture and Veterinary Medicine, but help me stay close to You who own the cattle on a thousand hills! Somebody called You the Lamb of God!

Lord, I do want to do my best in Geology, but I also must remember that You are my cornerstone and the Rock of my Salvation! Oh, I want to be outstanding in English and Journalism, but I will still realize that You are the primary protagonist in the greatest story ever told. I want the best grades in Pre-Law, but let me never neglect You—the Lawyer who never lost a case! Through You I can be outstanding in counseling, but I must remember You who is a heart-fixer and mind regulator! I plan to study hard in Music, but not lose sight of the fact that You are the only reason why Handel wrote the Messiah! And finally, Lord, Technology, but let me not forget that if I wait upon You, Lord, I shall renew my strength! I shall mount up on wings as eagles! I shall run and not be weary; I shall walk and not faint.

—CHRIS JACKSON

Chris Jackson is currently serving as campus minister at the American Baptist College and Tennessee State University in Nashville, Tennessee. He received his doctorate of ministry degree, with a concentration in youth ministry.

FOR ALL THOSE IN AUTHORITY—BOTH SECULAR AND SPIRITUAL

Father, in obedience to your Word, I pray for all men everywhere who have not heard the Full gospel that Christ still saves, heals, and delivers today. I thank You for sending forth laborers to share Jesus with them, and I bind the powers of darkness over the minds of those who have an opportunity to hear the message of salvation this day.

Father, I lift up to You the leaders of our nation, of the world, and all those who have secular authority over us, particularly our president, vice president, governor, mayor, senators, congressmen, and other government officials who have the judicial care of our cities, states, and nation.

I pray for all those who provide service and protection for the people of this country, such as our law enforcement officers, firefighters, school board authorities, teachers, and principals. I pray that these people have continual wisdom, knowledge, direction, and understanding regarding the decisions they are called to make on behalf of the people. I pray that their decisions are sound, fair and impartial, and in line with your Word that we may live a quiet and peaceable life in all goodliness and honesty.

I pray for the leaders in the Body of Christ and their families. I pray that they will continually have the Spirit of wisdom, revelation, and knowledge of your Word as they minister to your people the Word of Life. I pray that they will be strengthened with all might by your Spirit in the inner man, and that the Church will be on one accord— with one spirit, one mind, serving You.

I pray that believers throughout the world will come into the unity of the faith and into the fullness and stature of Christ, so that the world may see Jesus in us, and that You will be forever glorified in His Name. We pray this prayer in the wonderful name that is above all names, the Name of Jesus.

—DR. FREDERICK K. C. PRICE

In 1990, Dr. Price founded Fellowship of Inner City Work of Faith Ministries in Los Angeles, California. The organization's purpose is to spread the faith message among independent ministries in the metropolitan areas of the United States.

A Prayer for Good Government

Dear Lord, You have blessed our government down through the years. I have read where You made David King. We believe You gave us a leader in the last election. Now, dear Lord, as we approach this new election we need Your help. We believe that You give power to men and You take it away. Leaders are given power at Your command. Raise up men and women of God who will submit to Your Sovereignty and who will rule according to Your will. Please give us the national leaders we need to lead us into the 21st Century.

Amen.

—Reverend C. L. Smith

Reverend C. L. Smith is the minister of Pillar Rock Missionary Baptist Church in Houston, Texas. This prayer acknowledges the very real presence of God in our daily lives and the need to include Him in every aspect of our lives.

A Prayer for Our Leaders

Our Great and Almighty God, to You we pray. We thank You for being a God who leads us through the trials and tribulations of life. We thank You for being a God who doesn't leave us to our own devices, but provides a plan for us to follow. We thank You, for the leadership that You have provided through Your servants. Lord, we only ask that You continue to place in positions of authority those who will seek first Your kingdom and Your will. Bless our current leadership and the leadership to come. Help us to be willing and dedicated followers of those who are following after You. In the name of one who leads us daily in the paths of righteousness; in the name of Jesus we pray.

Amen.

—Reverend Chestina Mitchell Archibald

This prayer is based on a concept expressed in Isaiah 9:15a: "The ancient and honorable, he is the head." We ask God to send us leaders who are interested in His ways, who will perform their duties with righteousness and use their positions of authority positively to influence others.

PRAYER FOR ALL LEADERS

Father, we pray for the right election of our leaders throughout the world. Those whose hearts are filled with love and are inspired by you each day to do what is right for humanity. Those who ask your guidance every step of the way and are channels of peace. We pray for and declare peace on earth by reaching out and blessing all the people of the world with love and peace. That each inhabitant of every nation will be spiritually awakened and exercise patience and understanding with their fellow man.

We radiate peace and love with all those with whom we come in contact. We see the world with eyes of love regardless of what is happening. We give thanks for the wonderful changes that are taking place. Lord, let peace and love begin with us. Thank You, Father.

—REVEREND CARMEN YOUNG

In I John 4:7, the Gospel says: "Beloved, let us love one another: for love is of God." Reverend Young's reference to this verse reflects that, despite the various roles each of us plays, we all share God's love equally. We ask for God's help in providing us with leaders who are motivated by His will and who are concerned with what is right for all humanity.

FOR THOSE IN THE ARMED SERVICES
TO SAY

Lord, I am here on a battlefield in the midst of a war purportedly being fought for peace, democracy, and justice. Lord, I want love and harmony to prevail for all. Yet, I fear at this time for my own life. Make me courageous as I remember that there is no life except in You. Therefore, at this time I say to Thee, I surrender.

Use me now, Lord, even at this moment and this place to help bring Your kingdom here on earth. Strengthen me to help Your people know that we must love our neighbors as ourselves. Use me at this time to bring honor and glory to Thy name. In the holy and precious name of Jesus, I pray.

Amen.

—REVEREND CHESTINA MITCHELL ARCHIBALD

While those in the military are often placed in positions that require them to go against what they truly believe for the purpose of achieving a peaceful outcome, God will fill them with the courage to endure and the strength to uphold His name. As we are reminded in Proverbs 3:30: "Strive not with a man without cause, if he have done thee no harm."

PRAYER FOR THOSE IN THE ARMED FORCES

O mighty and magnificent God, I come right now on behalf of a loved one who has been called by our government to protect the nation in which we live. Lord, I do not understand why we, Your creatures, cannot live in harmony with each other. Even more tragic is seeing nations against nations, families against families, sisters against sisters, and brothers against brothers.

God, protect not only my loved one, but all persons listed in the armed services. Let my loved one be drawn closer to Thee, put your arms around my loved one, and let him/her be shielded with Your armor from head to toe. Then, O Lord, let him/her come back to us, improved in mind, body, and spirit. In the precious name of Jesus, I pray.

Amen.

—REVEREND CHESTINA MITCHELL ARCHIBALD

Reverend Archibald was inspired by Psalms 46:9a when writing this prayer: "He maketh war to cease unto the end of the earth." While we all look to the day when there will be no war, when people can live side by side in harmony, we look to God to protect those who have been sent to fight for our country, and ask Him to send our loved ones home safely.

PRAYER FOR A LOVED ONE IN THE ARMED FORCES

Perfect God of all creation, Holy God, the Omnipotent Lord, blessings, strength, and honor to your great name. Certainly, dear Lord, you know your sheep and where they are. You know where my loved one is. Whether in the States training, traveling to another military installation, or seeking peace on foreign soil, protect my loved one from the perils which confront the soldiers. Grant physical, mental and spiritual strength in times of weariness. In moments of anxiety and fear, give comfort and assurance with your Holy presence. Bring to their minds the love and care you possess for them and the love of family and friends behind.

As your will is done, we pray that restoration and reconciliation soon come to pass. In King Jesus's name we lift this petition.

Amen.

—REVEREND DARREN WHITE

When someone we love joins the armed forces, we may experience a whirlwind of emotions, from sadness to worry to loneliness. We can send our prayers for our loved ones to God, that He might watch over them closely and bring them home safely, comforting them with His eternal presence.

Psalm 8: Even as I Sleep Tonight

Raleigh, NC: Central Prison

O God my God
even as I sleep tonight
inside a cold steel cell
I feel the comfort of thy warmth
through my faith in thee
I dream of freedom
and an end to the oppression of people
I dream of worldwide peace
and the establishment of a universal brotherly
and sisterly love now on earth
as I awake to the morning dawn
liberated through thy grace and power
I will continue to keep the faith.

—Reverend Dr. Benjamin F. Chavis, Jr.

A longtime civil rights activist, Dr. Chavis is currently serving as the national convener of the National African American Leadership Summit (NAALS)—an umbrella group of approximately three hundred national, regional, and local black leaders. As former executive director and CEO of the NAACP, he was the youngest person ever to head the nation's oldest and largest civil rights organization. This prayer is taken from *Psalms from Prison*, a book of powerful prayers that speaks directly to the issues relevant to the experience of African Americans.

PSALM 4: GIVE ME THY PROTECTION

Raleigh, NC: Central Prison

Give me thy protection, O God
in the midst of my humiliation
while I am savagely stripped naked
by the standard operating procedure
of prison inhumanity
attempting to enslave
my mind, body, and spirit
protect me from the torture
that rages from cell to cell
destroying the fruit of thy creation
protect me from the voltage
of an electrical shock treatment at my body
protect me from the horror
of a behavior modification scalpel at my brain
and protect me, O God
from the institutional evil
that lurks behind the high walls of central prison
to a melody of human screams.

—REVEREND DR. BENJAMIN F. CHAVIS, JR.

Among his many exceptional accomplishments, Dr. Chavis was the executive director and CEO of the Commission for Racial Justice of United Church of Christ for eight years. He received his bachelor of arts degree in chemistry from the University of North Carolina, his master of divinity degree, magna cum laude, from Duke University, and his doctor of ministry degree from Howard University. This prayer was taken from *Psalms from Prison*.

A Prayer for Prisoners

O God of heaven and earth. Thank you for patience, thank you for forgiveness. Lord, I worship you, I praise you, I magnify your name. I thank you God for being the creator of time and the God of a second chance. God, I'm grateful that you are the only one and true judge and that you rule by grace and always grant us mercy. Thank you, God, for being God all by yourself. Thank you for teaching me how to worship you in spite of circumstances and situations. Lord, I trust you for direction, for peace, for joy, and freedom beyond all understanding. I thank you God that in the midst of confinement I am free. I thank you God that I am not conformed to this world but I'm transformed by the renewal of my mind and spirit. Now Lord, I praise you for the ability to make good decisions. Lord, if it be thy will, I pray that these prison doors be opened like you did for Paul and Silas, that I might be released to let my life shine in the world, that it might be a light to others.

—Desi Smith

A resident of Nashville, Tennessee, Desi Smith is a prison minister currently serving at the Faith, Hope and Love Fellowship. She previously worked for *Billboard* magazine, and now, in addition to her prison ministry, she is a publicist for many recording artists. Her prayer reminds us that although people in prison may have committed serious wrongdoings in the past, we must pray that they may recognize God and be reborn, anxious to find redemption.

A PRAYER ABOUT PEOPLE IN PRISON

Precious God of the Universe, I pray for all my brothers and sisters incarcerated. Lord, I pray for their strength. I pray for their families that are affected by their absence—parents, spouses, sons and daughters. Lord, I pray for those who are going before the parole boards, and for babies born behind prison walls. Lord, I pray that they will come to a realization of who you are and that you hold the real keys to their freedom. So now, Lord, touch the many prison facilities all over the world: touch the administrators, touch the guards, touch the teachers inside these walls. I pray, Lord, for many who have tried many things, that you send workers into this harvest to teach and preach your word, and to let these persons know that they have been created for greatness, and that in you, God, they are new creatures. Hear now my prayer, O Lord, I pray.

Amen.

—DESI SMITH

A single mother raising two young adults, Desi Smith is also extremely active in the community. In this prayer, she recognizes the value of every person and demonstrates our need to show mercy for all.

FOR PERSONS IN PRISONS AND JAILS

God of Freedom and Justice:

Our hearts are heavy as we remember those who are in prisons and jails throughout America. We lift them into your presence right now, O God, for your blessing. Help them to know that you are fully present with them, that you love them completely, and that your intention for each of them is freedom and the abundant life. Give those who are imprisoned justly the grace to repent of their wrong-doing, and sustain hope in those imprisoned unjustly for a new and better future.

We too repent, Lord, for our sins and shortcomings. We know that our homes, our neighborhoods, and our nation have often failed to surround each boy and girl with daily love as well as with daily bread. We have often let love of money loom larger than love of children, and have neglected to teach each child the Christian way by both word and example. Forgive us, Lord, and set us about the urgent task of Christian nurture for every child born into our midst.

Give us wisdom and courage to confront injustice in our society, Lord. The poor often get second-rate justice at the hands of police and courts. Help us to change the situation, Lord, so that everyone receives fair and just treatment, not harshness and disrespect. The psalmist tells us that "For all who are mistreated, the Lord brings justice." (Ps. 103:6) We claim that as a promise today, Lord. Lighten the burden and cheer the hearts of all prisoners and those who love them. We pray in the name of Jesus Christ, who even on the cross told a penitent prisoner, "I promise that today you will be with me in Paradise." (Lk. 23:43)

Amen.

—DR. FRED CLOUD

Dr. Cloud has worked extensively in the area of human rights, including a twenty-year period during which he served as executive director of the Metro Human Relations Commission in Nashville, Tennessee, and then taught at the University of Oklahoma from 1974 to 1981. He received his B.A., master of divinity, and doctor of ministry degrees from Vanderbilt University and his M.A. degree from Scarritt College.

Say Amen!

PRAYER FOR PERSONS WHO ARE
MENTALLY ILL

Dear God, My Lord and Savior, in the name of Jesus Christ your son, I am asking for your guidance and help. Jesus said, "Come unto me, all ye that labor and are heavy laden, and I will give you rest" (Matt. 11:28). I believe those words to be true and I know that you alone have the power to correct anything that is not in divine order. This is why I come before you now.

I pray that you will quiet my mind from the storm of despair and hopelessness that I presently feel, and I pray that you will restore the internal balance and harmony that has continued to elude me. I am failing in my struggle to break free from the shackles of self-doubt and isolation, and I am growing weary in my efforts to continually hold on to the belief that I will someday find some relief from this mental distress which I experience so painfully.

Look with favor upon me, Oh Lord, and know that I am open to receiving your direction and guidance. Move mightily within me and nourish my impoverished spirit so that I may grow in strength for the journey that lies ahead. Restore my inner vision and help me to re-discover the road whose path will lead me to a place of inward calm and resolve. Help me to identify the circumstances which brought such a mental burden on me, and give me the strength to resist falling prey to and feeling incapacitated by distress of such magnitude and force. Help me to identify the resources on which I can rely as I journey to get back on course, and give me the patience, persistence and stamina to stay strong and always in pursuit of an inner peace and spiritual symmetry.

Help me to rest in the knowledge that I have shared my burden with you and feel comforted in the belief that you will hear and honor my petition. I ask these things of you, in the name of Jesus Christ, Your Son, Our Lord, as I do know and believe that through you, all these things are possible.

—WILLIAM D. PARHAM, PH.D., AND SABRINA O. PARHAM, J.D.

William Parham has been a licensed psychologist for the past sixteen years, helping people to overcome life's challenges by teaching them to recognize their inner strengths and talents. His wife, Sabrina, is an accomplished attorney equally committed to assisting people in need. The couple, who reside in Los Angeles, not only share the mutual goal of someday working as a team, but also share "a marriage centered by God and grounded in a solid foundation of trust and reverence for each other."

For Those in Search of Employment

Lord, we are too blessed to be stressed. We know that You have a divine purpose for each of our lives; we seek to discover that purpose today. As we begin searching for careers, we start first by seeking Your guidance and Your blessing on the search. Touch those with whom we interview that they receive us in the Spirit of Christ. Help us, Lord, not to give way to disappointment, but to look at rejection as Your guidance to the occupation that You desire for us. Lord, teach us to turn every block into a stepping stone. And once hired, Lord, help us to work in a manner pleasing to our employer. We trust, Lord, that if we just depend on Your guidance and do our best, You will do the rest. In Jesus' name we pray.

　　Amen.

—Reverend Chestina Mitchell Archibald

Because of the competitiveness of today's job market, many people have difficulty in finding suitable employment. Reverend Archibald offers the following biblical verse as a source of her inspiration in writing this prayer: "That ye submit yourselves unto such, and to everyone that helpeth with us and laboureth" (2 Corinthians I:II).

Prayer for Those Who Are Retired to Say

Lord, I have come this far by believing, trusting, and learning in and through You. Even though many times I did not know what You wanted me to do, you led me, you guided me in ways and to places that I knew not. But each time, I found that Your way was above my way, and Your thought above my thought. Therefore, God, as I come to this point in my life's journey, I surrender myself anew to Thee, thanking You that I am still in my right mind, and that I have a reasonable portion of my health and most of the other amenities in life. Lord, You have been my stronghold in the past, and I rest in the assurance that You are the same God that was with me in my yesterdays, and that shall be with me in my tomorrows.

In the loving and precious name of Jesus, I pray.

Amen.

—Reverend Chestina Mitchell Archibald

As we mature and enter into our later stages in life, it is important to give thanks to God for guiding us thus far, remembering that He has been the one who gave us the strength to persevere. In Psalms 126:5, we are reminded that in the end, all of the hardships we have endured will not have been in vain: "They that sow in tears shall reap in joy."

For People with HIV/AIDS

Dear God, you are my comforter, confidant, and hope. I come to you, Lord, for with you I can be totally free. In you, I seek peace from physical pain in this body that no longer feels like mine. In you, Lord, I seek a peace that surpasses my understanding and gives me relief from physical pain, emotional distress, and spiritual disconnectedness. Ease my burdens of living with HIV/AIDS, Lord, as only you can do. Give me a calm, quiet spirit in the midst of this struggle. Unto you, Lord, I give my spirit, for you are my hope and joy. I love you, Lord. Unto you, I place my trust, today, tomorrow, and always.

    Amen.

—Reverend Meriann Taylor

Reverend Taylor is resident psychotherapist at Blanton-Peale Counseling Center in New York City. In addition, she is a faculty member of the Pastoral Studies Program and Pastoral Care Awareness Program at Blanton-Peale.

ABOUT PEOPLE AFFECTED BY HIV/AIDS

Precious Lord, my heart is heavy and my spirit is burdened. In you, Lord, I put my trust as I come seeking strength to support [say name of loved one here] in this war with HIV/AIDS. Give me your peace, Lord God. Give me your wisdom so my words, thoughts, and actions are acceptable to you. Increase my faith to believe that you are still God, even when I feel otherwise.

Amen.

—REVEREND MERIANN TAYLOR

Aside from her work at Blanton-Peale Counseling Center, Reverend Taylor is a consultant to the Arthur Ashe Institute for Urban Health in Brooklyn, New York. Her prayer deals with a very real and very serious problem in society today—a problem that may already affect you or someone you know.

A Prayer for One's Special Friends

Lord, I thank You for many dear friends. When I think of what a friend I have in dear Jesus, none can compare. Yet, You have sent me many others to help me travel through this life, being fulfilled in every way.

Lord, help me to live in Your spirit, that those who You have placed in my life will be strengthened. As they seek to bless me, Lord, may they in turn be blessed. When they seek to give me love, money, or service, let them prosper. If in our traveling together, Lord, any should turn and want to injure me, may they contract my love for You, God, and be healed. In the Holy and precious name of Jesus, I pray.

    Amen.

—Reverend Chestina Mitchell Archibald

Friends can be the most valuable thing one has in this lifetime, and it is important to acknowledge thanks to God for the love and joy these people have added to one's life. However, it is also important to keep sight of who our best friend truly is, as we are reminded in Proverbs 18:24: "He that maketh many friends doeth it to his own destruction; but there is a friend that sticketh closer than a brother."

A PRAYER TO HELP FRIENDS IN THEIR FAITH

Lord, I have friends who do not know You as their personal Lord and Savior. Please, God, touch my friends that they may find the peace, love, joy, and happiness that only comes from serving Thee.

In Jesus' name, I pray.

Also, Lord, help me to be a friend worthy of trust. May I alway be loyal to those who allow me the privilege of participating in their lives. Help me always to be honest and fair, allowing them to be themselves while I seek to love them unconditionally.

Amen.

—REVEREND CHESTINA MITCHELL ARCHIBALD

True friendship can be one of life's greatest treasures. The friends we make may not always share the same religious beliefs as us, but we pray that they may one day know God as we do. With God's help, one can be someone who is loyal, trustworthy, caring, and always present in times of need: the type of person described in Proverbs 17:17: "A friend loveth at all times. . . ."

Prayers for the Family

Here ye the word of the Lord. O house of Jacob, and all
the families of the house of Israel: Thus saith the Lord.
What inequity have your fathers found in me, that they
are gone far from me, and have walked after vanity,
and are become vain?

JEREMIAH 2:4–5

Except the Lord build the house, they labour in
vain that build it.

PSALMS 127:1a

THE GIFT OF THE FAMILY

God, we pray that you will give unto us, on this day, the remembrance of the value of the family and all that it is and will become as the foundation for the development and nurture of the human personality. Help us to know that family is a gift from you and that it is through your spirit that we can readily see and appreciate what the family offers to those who compose it.

We thank you for some of the experiences the family provides and even for the ones that are yet to come. We thank you for the mystery of love and the certainty of trust that is always available. We thank you for the gift of touch which comforts and cares when needed and the sacrifices made when least expected. We thank you for your spirit's presence in the minds of parents who attempt to train and guide and constantly pray that the highest good will come from what they have tried to do with and for their children. It is because of your gift of the family to us that life does impart meaning and purpose in our strivings to live creatively and responsibly with each other. We thank you for this wondrous gift and that you continue to tutor us in the magnificence of its reality, for without it we could not survive.

Amen.

—REVEREND DR. DONALD SCAVELLA

Commenting on his prayer, Reverend Scavella, of the United Methodist Union in Detroit, Michigan, says: "This prayer is a reflection of my past experiences in the home that was full of learning and nurturing. My parents gave me the freedom to express my creativity and to emerge as a positive self among other members of my family. These early years of training and guidance, tempered with unconditional care and concern, are still very much a part of who I am and who I am becoming."

A Prayer for One's Kindred

O God, who art more than an anthropomorphic projection of man, Thou who art Father, Mother, brother, and sister, our all and all, we thank You for blessing us with those closest to us. We thank You for fathers who have accepted Your example of fatherhood, and nurturing mothers who have heard Your call and seen Your examples of motherhood. We thank You, Lord, for our families from whom we learn what is meant by unconditional love. Thanks for our families from whom we learn how to truly support one another, for it is from our earthly families that we learn what it means to be a family in the body of Christ. We can only thank You for such blessings, and ask that we are as much a blessing to our families as they are to us. In the name of Jesus, our brother, in Your family, we pray.

Amen.

—Reverend Chestina Mitchell Archibald

This prayer was inspired by Genesis 2:23a: "This is now bone of my bones, and flesh of my flesh. . . ." We must thank the Lord not only for providing us with a family here on earth who loves us unconditionally, but for God our Father and Mother above, who set the perfect, holy example for all families to follow.

A PRAYER FOR WEDDING VOWS

Eternal God,

I come before you with a hopeful heart. Today, many get divorced and break their vows of matrimony. Others vow to follow Jesus, only to be found wandering in the wilderness. Lord, please give me divine strength to uphold any vows I utter before Thee. I offer now my marriage vows and spiritual vows to You for protection. I dwell no more on them—for they are in Your hands and all is well.

In Christ's Name, I pray.

Amen.

—REVEREND CHESTINA MITCHELL ARCHIBALD

In Romans 7:1a, 2, 4b, it is written, "Know ye . . . that the law hath dominion over a [person] as long as he liveth . . . that ye should be married . . . even to him who is raised from the dead, that we should bring forth fruit unto God." In today's society, it seems as if there are more broken marriages than ones that survive. We must realize that every relationship will encounter difficulties from time to time, but with God's love and guidance, we can stay faithful to the vows we took before Him, allowing our marriage to grow and thrive.

PRAYER FOR A HUSBAND-TO-BE

Dear God,

I am a young man who has found the woman whom I want to make my wife. I desire to be the best husband she could ever have, yet I have few examples to emulate. The families that seem healthy on the surface also have many underlying problems. Lord, help me to do my part of being a husband so well that if problems arise, they can be immediately solved, because as the head of the household, I trust in and depend on You. If there is a pattern of a true, healthy family in this community that is pleasing to You, place it in my path so that I might observe it and learn. In Jesus's name I pray.

Amen.

—REVEREND CHESTINA MITCHELL ARCHIBALD

In Hebrews 13:4, we are told: "Marriage is honorable in all." Looking at society today, it may be difficult to see examples of God's will being carried out; many people don't take their marriage vows seriously, and others neglect their responsibilities to their families. With God's help, however, one can find the strength to do as He wishes, creating a home filled with love, respect, and trust.

A PRAYER ABOUT HUSBANDS

Our Heavenly Father,
You've allowed us to be endowed by your presence and we say thank
you. By your grace, please be gracious in your blessings upon the
husbands of today. Father, please allow all husbands to be mindful
of the building process of your kingdom. Allow them to have the
understanding of your will. Allow them to be honest in their emotions. Allow them to be trustful in their passion toward their wives.
Allow them to be able to communicate, respect and be loyal in their
dealings of the home and family. O Lord, grant I pray, that all
husbands be embodied with that love that flows from heart to heart,
soul to soul. And Father, in the giving and in thy blessings, be mindful of thy spirit, that praises thee, that adorns thee, that glorifies thee.
In the Name of Jesus,
    Amen.

—DR. JAMES WARREN

Dr. James Warren is currently director of juvenile services for the city of Vicksburg, Mississippi. His prayer reflects on all the qualities in a husband that are
necessary in helping a marriage to thrive and filling a home with love and strength.

Help My Wife and Me Through This Troubling Time

Lord, I come to You with a broken heart. I have done everything that I know how to do to make my wife happy, yet it seems to be to no avail. I am confused and feel lonely even when we are together.

I am a man who has tried very hard to understand my wife in order that our relationship can be strengthened, but it seems that every time I make one step forward, she takes two back. Then Lord, I know that she often feels the same way. Lord, I pray that You help us get in sync with one another, emotionally and spiritually. Help me to give and forgive more freely. Then help me to move out of self, so that You may enter my soul and help me accept my wife as she is, so that our relationship may be what You would have it be. Help us to march together in harmony with You. This I pray in Jesus' name.

Amen.

—Reverend Chestina Mitchell Archibald

Reverend Archibald was inspired by I Corinthians 7:14a, 15b in writing this prayer: "[T]he unbelieving husband is sanctified by the wife, and the unbelieving wife is sanctified by the husband . . . God hath called us to peace." Marriage is never easy, but in order to come to a deeper understanding of one's spouse, one must look to God for patience and strength.

LORD, THANK YOU FOR MY WIFE

Thank You, God, for my loving, patient, and kind wife. I am blessed with a beautiful, precious woman far beyond what I honestly feel I deserve. Help me, Lord, to be more considerate. Make me more trustworthy and supportive. Grant me all the attributes that will make her happy as we both come to Thee.

   Amen.

—REVEREND CHESTINA MITCHELL ARCHIBALD

Reverend Archibald offers Proverbs 18:22 as the motivation behind writing this prayer: "Who so findeth a wife findeth a good thing, and obtaineth favour of the Lord." It is important not only to show your wife your appreciation for her love and support, but also to thank God for blessing you with such a wonderful woman and devoted spouse.

A Prayer for Husbands

Dear God,

We live in a world that is patriarchal, where often men feel that their manhood is directly related to their ability to dominate and be in charge. Let those who have chosen to be united in holy matrimony with a woman realize that the strongest form of leadership is that which is guided by love, and that one is truly in charge when another submits out of utmost respect. Help men realize that there is a marked difference between a man and a husband. Lord, You have said in Your word that a husband is one who will lay down his life for his wife. Lord, help men become husbands. In Christ's name we pray.

Amen.

—Reverend Chestina Mitchell Archibald

In Ephesians 5:25, a comparison is made between the love of a husband for his wife and the love of Jesus for the church: "Husbands, love your wives, even as Christ also loved the church, and gave himself for it." This prayer reminds us that there is no place for power struggles in a marriage—instead, the love for one's spouse should be motivation enough to maintain a relationship based on equality and respect.

EVENING PRAYER
A Prayer for Husbands to Say

God you who are my father and my mother please protect my wife and children. If I should die before I wake help them to rebound, in the wake. Continue to form my wife spiritually so that she can continue to serve you unequivocally. Open the doorways to heaven for her and greet her with every step of her approach. Help her to keep her faith with all of life's trials, and convictions, let the sun never see her brilliance drained. She is a child of your creation, her assent to you has been her faith. Teach my daughters and sons this woman's character, wisdom, and spiritual dimensions. Teach my children to have my wife's self reliance and let their dependence be only in you.

Let all of their lives be lived for the glory of the kingdom, let their lives be lived for You! Let the faint-hearted sing. For here stands a wife and children, eminent, and bondage free.

—REVEREND TERRANCE HAYES

Reverend Hayes currently serves on the Board of Discipleship for the United Methodist Church in Nashville, Tennessee. Among his involvements, he continually seeks to expand the church and spread the word of God.

A Prayer for a Wife

As I search the scriptures, I see guidelines to being a good wife. I believe my husband is a gift from You, and I pray to be a dutiful, loving wife who can inspire him and support him in his daily life. In times of difficulty, let me be his resting place. Through me, let him be connected with Your feminine spirit of love, comfort, and steadiness. As his wife, let me feel from him Your masculine nature of strength, love, and solidity. I pray that each of us, at the appropriate times, will be able to transcend these traditional roles and just love each other as You love all humankind. Lord, help me to be a wonderful wife who brings out the greatness of my husband. Help me rear any children we may conceive in love. Lord, this is my choice. Never let me despise those who find their callings in other careers. Lord, help the love for my children to flow freely. Bind us together as a family. Thank You, Lord, for allowing me to be a wife to a man that is truly a husband. Help me to make our house a home.
In Christ's Name.

    Amen.

—REVEREND CHESTINA MITCHELL ARCHIBALD

The writing of this prayer was influenced by I Timothy 5:14: "I will therefore that the younger women marry, bear children, guide the house. . . ." A woman's place in the family is a special one, based on strength, love, and kindness—God can give one the courage and guidance to be the best wife and mother possible, as well as granting one the wisdom and faith to build a home where His will is always done.

HELP ME BE A LOVING AND SUPPORTIVE SPOUSE, LORD

Dear Lord of Union and Lord of Peace,
I come to You now with a heavy heart. My spouse and I had a big argument, and could not come to an understanding. I feel so angry I could fight, but I know that isn't right. My spouse probably feels the same about me. I hate to seem like a nagging wife, but he keeps doing the same irritating things over and over which I've asked him not to do. It seems like if he loved me he'd make an effort to please me by doing the simple things I ask him to do. And he never seems to appreciate what I do for him, no matter how hard an effort.

I guess You feel the same way towards me sometimes, don't you? I often ignore Your will or neglect the lovely efforts You make on my behalf. Excuse my self-centered attitude. Help me understand my spouse's heart, and to love him beyond what I perceive to be his limitations or shortcomings. Please help me to become a pool of love into which he can dive and swim freely. Please let my embracing love uplift my spouse and allow him to become a greater person. Please help us to become perfect complements, so that the two of us may become a sphere of love. Please let my spouse feel Your deep love every day of his life, in all that he does, so his heart can be open and joyous. Please forgive me for my inability to support my spouse at all times. Guide our relationship, and help us grow to be a couple who embodies Your highest qualities. Please help me to let go of my petty qualms, and to help me to support and love my spouse completely. Lord, thank You for Your guidance. In Christ's Name.
    Amen.

—REVEREND CHESTINA MITCHELL ARCHIBALD

This prayer deals with the conflicts that can arise in a marriage, and the way that we must forgive our spouse just as God forgives us when we lose sight of His will. We are reminded of the importance of unconditional love in a relationship, and pray to God for the ability to ignore unnecessary anger and to transcend petty frustrations in our quest for a harmonious union.

A PRAYER FOR A CHILDLESS COUPLE

Magnificent Lord, You know the deepest desires of our hearts. Give us a baby to love, hold, and cuddle. May we be granted the opportunity to train a child in reverent fear of Thee. Lord, I promise that if You give me a child, I will dedicate this child to You. We would like to have a child who is bone of our bones, and flesh of our flesh. Yet, Lord, we promise to love whatever child You see fit to place in this family. Thank You, Lord, for I know You have heard my prayer. Amen.

—REVEREND CHESTINA MITCHELL ARCHIBALD

In the writing of this prayer, Reverend Archibald was inspired by Psalms 127:3: "Lo, children are a heritage of the Lord; and the fruit of the womb is his reward." Although many couples desire a child born of their own blood, it is important for them to see God's blessing in the form of any child He may place into their home.

A Prayer for a Newborn

God of our weary years, God of our silent years, Thou who sustained us when hope unborn had died. It is to You, O Creator, who formed us in Your image, that Thou hast called forth this new life. Adorn this head with wisdom, and this little heart with love. Cause this child to move beyond the rimes of mediocrity to greatness. Strengthen this child to live up to her or his unlimited potential by following Your divine will and tapping into Your Holy power.

May this child always do what is pleasing in Thy sight. If ever faced with injustice, may she or he turn every block into a stepping stone. May she or he know that dignity does not come in receiving honors, but rather in deserving them. May she or he possess the pride and royalty of our heritage to transform generations yet unborn.

Lord, never let her or him become too pleased with herself or himself, because small dreams have been realized or too overjoyed because she or he arrived safely by sailing too close to the shore. Never let this little one become so engrossed with the abundance of things that she or he loses a thirst for the waters of life. Challenge each of us, Lord, to be an anchor of support for this little one, and each other, as this one dares to move boldly, to venture on wider seas where storms will show Your mastery, where losing sight of land, she or he will find the stars that give direction to Your will. In the name of Jesus Christ, we pray.

Amen.

—Reverend Chestina Mitchell Archibald

As we are reminded in Psalms 121:8, God is always watching over us: "The Lord shall preserve thy going out and thy coming in from this time forth, and even for evermore." We can rest easier knowing that each newborn child brought into the world is wrapped in God's love and protection, a recipient of His guidance and encouragement every step of the way.

PRAYER FOR THE BLACK CHILD

O God of Harriet Tubman and Sojourner Truth
of Frederick Douglass and Booker T. Washington
of George Washington Carver and Mary McLeod Bethune,
Be with Your Black sons and daughters today.

O God of Martin Luther King and Malcolm X
of James Baldwin and Fannie Lou Hamer
of Howard Thurman and Benjamin Mays,
Be with Your Black children today.

—MARIAN WRIGHT EDELMAN

An advocate for disadvantaged Americans for her entire professional career, Marian Wright Edelman is probably best known as the founder and president of the Children's Defense Fund (CDF)—an organization devoted to educating the nation about the needs of children and trying to prevent young people from dropping out of school, getting pregnant, or getting into trouble. An author of several books, she is a graduate of Spelman College and Yale Law School.

Prayers for All Our Children

O God of all children of Somalia, Sarajevo, South Africa, and South
    Carolina
Of Albania, Alabama, Bosnia, and Boston,
Of Cracow and Cairo, Chicago and Croatia,
Help us to love and respect and protect them all.

O God of Black and Brown and White and Albino children and all
    those mixed together,
Of children who are rich and poor and in between,
Of children who speak English and Spanish and Russian and
    Hmong and languages our ears cannot discern,
Help us to love and respect and protect them all.

O God of the child prodigy and the child prostitute,
of the child of rapture and the child of rape,
Of runaway or thrown-away children who struggle every day without
    parent or place or friend or future.
Help us to love and respect and protect them all.

O God of children who can walk and talk and hear and see and sing
    and dance and jump and play and
of children who wish they could but can't,
Of children who are loved and unloved, wanted and unwanted,
Help us to love and respect and protect them all.

O God of beggar, beaten, abused, neglected, homeless, AIDS, drug,
    and hunger-ravaged children,
Of children who are emotionally and physically and mentally fragile,
and of children who rebel and ridicule, torment and taunt,
Help us to love and respect and protect them all.

O God of children of destiny and despair, of war and of peace,
Of disfigured, diseased, and dying children,
Of children without hope and of children with hope to spare and to
    share,
Help us to love and respect and protect them all.

—MARIAN WRIGHT EDELMAN

Marian Wright Edelman began her exceptional career in the mid-1960s when, as the first black woman admitted to the Mississippi bar, she directed the NAACP Legal Defense and Educational Fund office in Jackson, Mississippi. Some of her other notable accomplishments include founding the Washington Research Project, a public interest law firm and the parent body of the Children's Defense Fund, and serving as counsel for the Poor People's March that Martin Luther King, Jr., began organizing before his death.

PRAYER FOR THE CHILDREN

Spirit of God, come into our hearts and make us sensitive to the needs of our children. In the face of life's mysteries and its vast imponderables, give us renewed faith to undertake and embrace our children, whose needs are far greater than our own.

Keep us alert and visionary as we keep our children at the very center of our lives. As they continue to grow and become responsible men and women, and as they find their rightful places in society, may we offer them hope for the facing of an unknown tomorrow.

We ask thy mercy in Jesus' name.
     Amen.

—Dr. Clyde A. Anderson

Residing in New York, Dr. Anderson is area executive secretary for East and Central Africa at The General Board of Global Ministries of the United Methodist Church. On his prayer, he says: "I believe in children and their future. They are the center of my joy, and cause me to be proactive in my stance against the evils of society which may impede their personal and professional development."

GENERATIONAL PRAYER

O Gracious heavenly parent, we gather to honor our ancestors who through their great works of fighting for equality, have sought to expose the greatness of Your ebony children by allowing the world to view faintly the deeper recesses of our spirituality, undergirded with human struggle. We have come forth as pure gold and all praises be to Thee.

Bless now, Lord, this generation. May we remember not only the living dead, but be motivated to prepare and make a better world for the living unborn. In Your Holy name, we pray.

Amen.

—REVEREND CHESTINA MITCHELL ARCHIBALD

The writing of this prayer was influenced by Leviticus 23:43: "That your generations may know that . . . I am the Lord your God." As we remember the greatness of those who have gone on before us, we ask God to bless the forthcoming generations, and to give us the wisdom and courage to build a better world for our children, as our ancestors did for us.

Prayer for Children

Almighty God, we come in the name of your Son, Jesus Christ, and in the power of the Holy Spirit, thanking and praising you for all our blessings: of life, family, friends, and enemies; thanking you for a portion of health, wealth, and peace; praising you most of all for Salvation, eternal life, and joy.

Eternal God, in your wisdom you have designed our very existence, and in your grace, you have loved us into life. In your goodness, O God, you have given us children and youth to care for—we thank you. And in your mercy you have given instructions on love, nurturance, and care of these young people—we praise you.

Now God, we have failed to teach, guide, nurture, and care for our children as you have commanded, so we ask your forgiveness. O Divine One, we have allowed gangs, violence, and drugs to possess the very lives of our children. Forgive us for our apathy and give us courage, boldness, wisdom, and knowledge to reclaim our children for you.

Most merciful God, we come boldly now asking you to give us grace sufficient for our need to be better examples for our children and youth. Help us to grow in the knowledge of Jesus Christ so that as Christians we can help our children and youth to grow and live as you have commanded us. Open our eyes, hearts, and will to work out and meet the needs of these young ones; change us, so that we may help change them.

And gracious God, we thank you for the young ones who have given their lives to you and are reaching out to others. Give them more love, grace, and confidence to continue their journey in faith.

Then accept these our prayers so that we may come to know you more fully and love one another as you have loved us.

Amen.

—Reverend Dr. Rosa B. Clements

Among her many accomplishments, Dr. Clements has received the Clark Preaching Award, the Volunteer Services Award, and the Georgia Harkness Award. She has also been listed in *Who's Who in American Colleges and Universities*, and *Who's Who in Business and Professional Women*.

PRAYER FOR BOYS RAISED
WITHOUT FATHERS

Most Wise and Empowering God,

We come before you grateful for your fantastic power. We know that you find ways to give joy to the faint of spirit, courage to the recondite soul and forgiveness to those lost in sin. Lord, as we prostrate ourselves before you this day, we offer praise for the many blessings that you heap upon us. Your generosity knows no boundaries and your beneficence has no limits. We praise you that you find unusual ways of lifting your people to the glories that you alone provide.

God, we pray especially today for those boys who must learn to be men with no men in their home. Lord, bless them to discover models of manhood who honor your guidance and seek your direction. Give to them discerning souls and spiritual eyes that seek instruction from persons who love you and are called according to your purpose. By your grace, these boys can gain all that you covenant with them for. Let them keep their hopes stayed on you. Permit them to seek, first and foremost, to trust in you. Then they can vanquish any difficulty. Then they can succeed despite any obstacle. Help them to believe that they can do all things through Jesus Christ, who strengthens them. Then we, and they, will be careful to give you all of the praise, honor and glory. In the strong name of Jesus,

 Amen.

—Reverend Vance P. Ross

Reverend Ross is well known for his ability to help people to communicate effectively and positively, guiding them to realize their priorities and become spiritually empowered.

A PRAYER FOR ABUSED CHILDREN

God of Love and Justice,

We know that you stand against the injury and impairment of your people. There is no injustice that you excuse, no mischief that you condone. You are the Defender of the defenselsss, the Vindicator of the innocent. You do not hold weakness or youth against your people. You love them. You want happy lives for your children. Therefore, you do not favor those who use their strength to harm others. Your wrath is kindled against violation. You oppose purveyors of agony and anguish.

God, we ask that you surround those who know the pain of abuse with the helping touch of your hands. May they come to know that you are the God that is all righteous, just and fair. Give to these, your mistreated children, the joy of your resurrection promise, the promise that they shall soon conquer the distress that has unfairly beset them. Let them experience the exhilarating presence of your triumphant spirit. Give to them the marvelous assurance that they shall inherit your shalom, live in your harmony and indeed experience your joy.

In the name of Jesus we pray and by the power of the Spirit we dare to believe.

Amen.

—REVEREND VANCE P. ROSS

Reverend Ross is on the General Board of Discipleship of the United Methodist Church in Nashville, Tennessee. This prayer invokes both humility and joy, while petitioning God for protection and mercy.

CHILDREN'S PRAYERS

Thank You Lord for everything.
For the morning when I wake and the evening when I sleep. Thank
   You Lord.

Blessed are You O God, ruler of this world,
I thank You for the bread which comes from the seeds which grow
   in the earth You created.

Blessed are You O Lord,
Your strength and power fill the earth. For bringing this special time
   and the special things we enjoy.

O God, You are King.
You made the big and beautiful sea. The fruit of the tree and all the
   wonderful foods that we eat.

Blessed are You O God,
Who helps me when I am sad and when I am tired. Thank You for
   helping me.

O God, grant me peace, goodness, blessings, grace, kindness, and
   mercy. God, bless my mother and my father.

O God, my Lord, Jesus Christ, my Savior, and Holy Spirit, my guide,
   thank You for helping me in all I think, all I do, and all I say.

This is the day that You have made, O Lord. I will rejoice and be
   glad in it.

Now that the day has begun, I thank God for the sweet sleep with
   which He blessed me. Thank You for waking me up this
   morning. Help me to do the right things today, and give me the

strength to do the things I ought to do, and the courage to make wise decisions.

Take my hand and lead me today. May I be a blessing to all I meet. Bless those at home, at school, on the street, while I play and work. Take my hand and never let me stray. Be my guide in all I do and say. Hold me, Lord, lest I stray. I do not want to be alone. I need Your help. I need You, Lord.

We have this day before us. So before it is gone, help me to do all I can do, so today will not be a wasted day.

—REVEREND CHESTINA MITCHELL ARCHIBALD

Reverend Archibald was inspired by Luke 18:16 in the writing of this prayer: "Suffer little children to come unto me, and forbid them not: for of such is the Kingdom of God." It is important to teach young children about God and how much He loves us, so that they may develop a strong, unwavering faith as they grow into brave, honest, and loving adults, never losing sight of the One who is responsible for all of their blessings.

A PRAYER FOR MOTHERS

O Lord, we thank You for loving us unconditionally, we thank You for nurturing us, we thank You for Your discipline, and we thank You for being a God who raises us, Your children, with tender loving care. We also thank You, Lord, for the mothers You have blessed us with here on earth. They have demonstrated your unconditional love to us like no other. Please bless them and keep them. Strengthen them while convincing us to never fail to honor and cherish our mothers. In the name of Jesus, we pray.

Amen.

—REVEREND CHESTINA MITCHELL ARCHIBALD

We are reminded in Exodus 20:12: "Honour thy . . . mother: that thy days may be long upon the land which the Lord thy God giveth thee." In order to show our thanks to God for blessing us with such wonderful, loving mothers here on earth, we must express our love for our mothers daily by cherishing them and staying true to the beliefs they instilled in us.

THE 23RD PSALM
(Dedicated to Mother)

————

1. The Lord is my Shepherd, I have all I need,
She makes me lie down in green meadows,
Beside the still waters, She will lead.

2. She restores my soul, She rights my wrongs,
She leads me in a path of good things,
And fills my heart with songs.

3. Even though I walk, through a dark and dreary land,
There is nothing that can shake me,
She has said She won't forsake me,
I'm in Her hand.

4. She sets a table before me, in the presence of my foes,
She anoints my head with oil,
And my cup overflows.

5. Surely, surely goodness and kindness will follow me,
All the days of my life,
And I will live in Her house,
Forever, forever and ever.

6. Glory be to our Mother, and Daughter.
And to the Holy of Holies,
As it was in the beginning, is now and ever shall be,
World, without end. Amen.

—BOBBY McFERRIN

Bobby McFerrin is a highly acclaimed musician, known not only for his creative use of voice in jazz music but also for his growing reputation as a conductor of some of America's greatest orchestras. He has won ten Grammy awards and has collaborated with such artists as Herbie Hancock, Wayne Shorter, Chick Corea, and Yo Yo Ma. His adaptation of Psalm 23 was written for and dedicated to his mother.

A PRAYER ABOUT FATHERS

Lord God, as we look around today, we see that so many children are not having the opportunity to know their fathers. Help fathers to know and appreciate the role that You have ordained for them to play in the lives of their children. Then help them to assume responsibilities for the act of creation that brought these precious lives into being. Strengthen them to live moral lives, so that they may be models for their children. When they seek to discipline their children, let them do it in love. Let them not be the ones to provoke their own children to wrath. In Thy holy name, we pray.

Amen.

—REVEREND CHESTINA MITCHELL ARCHIBALD

This prayer is based on Exodus 20:12: "Honour they father . . . that thy days may be long upon the land which the Lord thy God giveth thee." In today's world, it is unfortunately common to find people who have grown up without a father. We ask God to give men who father children the courage to understand what it truly means to be a "father," and we thank God for blessing us with those fathers devoted to the fulfillment of His will on earth.

A FATHER'S PRAYER FOR MORNING

O God of power and God of might, O God of little girls' hair you
got them to church and you got them back and no one made any
    funny cracks
it's Monday morning and their mom's not back and their hair needs
    to be done again . . .
please give me the power, please give me the might to deal with these
    naps, knots, and dreads real
tight so that this little girl's hair will last at least till night. . . .

    Amen.

—REVEREND TERRANCE HAYES

Reverend Hayes is currently serving at St. Paul's United Methodist Church in San Antonio, Texas. In this prayer, the minister acknowledges the devoted fathers who are often overlooked.

A FATHER'S PRAYER

Dear loving God, Father to us all, I come at this time to seek Your guidance in rearing this child that You have placed in my charge. Lord, her energy is so high I often feel battered and worn, yet I dare not shirk from my responsibility. Therefore, God, not only do I seek Your guidance; I also ask that You grant me strength to run this race to see what the end will be.

Send harmony to dwell in this home. May I never get in the way of my child's ambition because of my limited vision. May I always know when to hold them, when to fold them, and when to walk away, letting You take complete control. Thanks, God, for granting me now Your peace as I let go and let You. In the precious name of Jesus the Christ, I pray.

   Amen.

—VERNON WINFREY

Vernon Winfrey is the father of television personality Oprah Winfrey. He served on the City Council of Nashville, Tennessee, for sixteen years, representing the Fifth District. He is also a professional barber who owns the Winfrey Barber Shop, located on Vernon Winfrey Avenue in Nashville. He is known as a friend to many.

PRAYER FOR MY SONS

Holy Father, how I praise and magnify your holy name! I know that you are worthy of all honor and praise, for you have been faithful to me and to my family all of our lives. I confess that we have not always been faithful to you, but you have forgiven and blessed us in spite of ourselves and I thank you.

Father, I present my sons to you. I ask that they will grow up whole, for whole is holy. I want them to be of a mind to praise you, to love you, to worship and adore you, for as long as you are primary in their lives, they will be strong, responsible Black men who are blessed to be a blessing.

Thank you, Father, for hearing your servant's prayer that is prayed in the precious name of my Lord and Savior, Jesus the Christ. Amen.

—MARJORIE L. KIMBROUGH

Marjorie Kimbrough is currently assistant professor of religion and philosophy at Clark Atlanta University in Atlanta, Georgia. Commenting on her prayer, she says: "This prayer reminds me of the gift of sons and the opportunities for them to be both blessed and a source of blessing. I have constantly prayed that my sons will be whole, holy."

LORD, HERE WE IS, MAYBE FOR THE LAST TIME
From *Native Son*

Lord, here we is, maybe for the last time. You gave me these children, Lord, and told me to raise 'em. If I failed, Lord, I did the best I could (*Ahmen!*) These poor children's been with me a long time and they's all I got. Lord, please let me see 'em again after the sorrow and suffering of this world! (*Hear her, Lawd!*) Lord, please let me see 'em where I can love 'em in peace. Let me see 'em again beyond the grave! (*Have mercy, Jesus!*) You said You'd heed prayer, Lord, and I'm asking this in the name of Your son.

—RICHARD WRIGHT (1908–1960)

Born on a plantation near Natchez, Mississippi, in 1908, Richard Wright was raised in Memphis, Tennessee. As a teenager, he decided to become a writer after "accidentally" coming across H. L. Mencken's *Book of Prefaces*. In 1934, he went to work in Chicago and became involved with the Federal Writers' Project as part of the Works Progress Administration. This prayer is an excerpt from his most acclaimed work, *Native Son* (1940, Harper & Row), the story of Bigger, a young black man confined by a white, racially prejudiced society, who ends up expressing his uncontrollable rage and bitterness in the form of violent acts. The prayer is said by Bigger's mother before he is about to be taken to jail for murder and rape.

PRAYER FOR SINGLE PARENTS

Lord, the phrase "single parent" is only appropriate when one does not acknowledge Thy presence in their lives. Otherwise, God, You are always there as that second parent. You are a father to the fatherless, and a mother to the motherless. You are a parent, a lover, and a friend. God, you reigned in the past, in the present, and shall reign in the future. Therefore, I now take hold to Your unchanging hand. I am now ready to soar through life with blessed assurance that Your goodness shall reign. I now accept wholeness of mind, body, and spirit for myself and my children, knowing that we are complete as a family unit because You dwell with us.

    Amen.

—REVEREND CHESTINA MITCHELL ARCHIBALD

Reverend Archibald cites Ephesians 6:1, 14 as the motivation in writing this prayer: "Obey your parents in the Lord: for this is right . . . wherefore take unto you the whole armour of God. . . . Stand . . . having your loins girt about with the truth." Raising a child alone is a difficult thing to do, but single parents must be aware that they are not alone—God is always standing beside them, ready to help, listen, protect, and love.

A Prayer on Divorce

Lord, I come before You this morning because I am alienated from the one who I thought would be my life companion. We entered as partners with You in the act of creation. Children have been born of our flesh, of our spirits, of our minds. I hurt to think that a bill of divorcement has been necessary because we could never come together before Thee, and certain events have tainted the relationship beyond reconciliation (unless a miracle takes place through You). Lord, who can heal all hurt, accept my plea to heal this ailing relationship. If reconciliation is to take place, clear my mind that I may forget all pain. If we are to remain apart, please grant us the strength to have a civil relationship for the sake of our children, and for all others who might be affected hereafter. This I ask in Jesus' name.

Amen.

—Reverend Chestina Mitchell Archibald

The theme of this prayer is found in Mark 10:4, 5: "And they . . . suffered to write a bill of divorcement . . . for the hardness of your heart." While ideally God desires for us to work out any differences we have within our marriages, sometimes a divorce is unavoidable. With God's help, those in the midst of a divorce can find the strength to carry on, and their pain can be healed more rapidly.

A GRANDPARENT'S PLEA FOR STRENGTH

Lord, I've raised my child and thought I was through and here I am
    with more.
I'm tired, I'm old, I'm broke and bent, I want to rest but can't.
My child is lost to drink and drugs, young flesh and blood needs
    love and care.
Lord, give me strength to do Your will and raise my grandchild well.

—MARIAN WRIGHT EDELMAN

Because of her phenomenal work as an advocate for people everywhere in need, Marian Wright Edelman has been the recipient of many honors, such as the Albert Schweitzer Humanitarian Prize, and she was also a MacArthur Foundation Prize Fellow. A graduate of Spelman College, she served on the college's Board of Trustees, acting as chairperson from 1976 until 1987.

A PRAYER FOR FAMILY

Heavenly Father, I intercede continually for my family and relatives. I pray for my father, mother, sisters, brothers, aunts, uncles, cousins, and in-laws. I thank You for sending forth laborers to share Jesus with those who have a need to be filled with the Holy Spirit, healed and living godly lives according to Your Word. I bind the powers of darkness over their thoughts and minds and over anything that would try to stop them from receiving their spiritual needs. I cast the care upon You of those who need to respond to the witness of the Holy Spirit concerning Jesus in their lives, but who have chosen not to respond—because I know You care for them more than I do (name those who have special needs). And I thank You for it, Father.

I pray continually for all the saints and servants of God. I pray that as they hear the Word, they will be doers of Your Word and not just hearers only. That they will continue to sincerely desire the milk of the Word that they may grow in grace and in the knowledge of Your will and of Your Word, that the eyes of their understanding will be enlightened daily, and that they may make right decisions in their lives so that they may be blameless in Your presence. I pray that they walk in the Spirit and that they shall not fulfil the lusts of the flesh, that they lead holy lives, that they walk in divine health, divine prosperity and that all their needs are met according to Your riches in glory by Jesus Christ.

I intercede on behalf of my husband (or wife) continually. I thank You that he (or she) has the wisdom to make right decisions that he (or she) needs to make this day. I thank You for protecting him (or her) from any voice or spirit that is not of You.

I pray continually for our home. I thank You for a godly home, a godly husband (or wife) and for godly children. I thank You that because we have made You, Father God, the most high, our habitation, no evil shall befall us and no plague shall come nigh our dwelling, because You give Your angels charge over us to keep us in all of our ways. We are blessed as a family because we fear You and delight greatly in Your commandments; therefore, our seed shall be mighty upon the earth and they (name your children) shall be blessed. I thank You that our children have the wisdom to make every decision they need to make today; in their home, in their marriage, in rearing their children and on their jobs, our young ones will serve You all the days of their lives because this is a family that is set apart to serve You until Jesus comes. In Jesus' name, I pray.

Amen.

—DR. BETTY R. PRICE

Dr. Price, whose husband is pastor of Crenshaw Christian Center in Los Angeles, is founder of the church's alcohol-drug abuse program and the twenty-four-hour Intercessory Prayer Network. Every Thursday night, she holds an old-fashioned prayer meeting for those who are likeminded.

A PRAYER ABOUT FAMILY

O God, reveal to us our true family. May we understand that every child of Yours is a child of ours. May we understand that we are all part of the same family because we are one in spirit. Throughout our history, Lord, family has included members brought to us out of circumstance rather than by blood. May we always hold this concept dear as we remember Jesus' question: *Who is my mother? Who is my brother?—He who doeth the will of the Father.*

   Amen.

—REVEREND CHESTINA MITCHELL ARCHIBALD

In Deuteronomy 7:6, we are reminded that our family consists not only of our blood relatives, but of anyone who follows the will of God: "For thou art a holy people unto the Lord thy God, and the Lord hath chosen thee to be a peculiar people unto himself above all the nations that are upon the earth."

Prayers for Special Events and Occasions

Trust in the Lord with all thine heart; and lean not unto
thine own understanding. In all thy ways acknowledge Him,
and He shall direct thy paths.

PROVERBS 3:5–6

A PRAYER IN PRAISE OF LEADERSHIP

O Gracious, Almighty, Eternal and Omniscient God,

We come to bid one farewell who has done much for the upbuilding of this institution. In a time when it appeared to the naked eye that all hope was gone, You worked through this leader.

As we take this time to express our gratitude for work well done, we ask that You not only bless this occasion, but continue to bless this organization and all associated herewith.

Guide us as we continue to reach higher heights where all may know that Your presence abides here. Let all who come here, or come in contact with those who have journeyed here, know this is no ordinary place because You have made it special. Make the great works of this leader be remembered forever. In Christ's name.
Amen.

—REVEREND CHESTINA MITCHELL ARCHIBALD

Reverend Archibald wrote this prayer for a farewell celebration for Dr. Henry Ponder, former president of Fisk University. The prayer offers thanks to God for blessing us with exceptional leaders who are motivated by His will.

A Prayer for a Young Woman's Birthday

Lord, all I am and hope to be,
I humbly offer, King, to thee!
When clouds arise, thy guidance send,
Accept my life, and bless it, Friend.

When I was but a tiny child,
Thou shielded me from tempests wild;
And gave me strength to do the right
Within temptation's treacherous sight.

And now in girlhood's solemn time
Oh, make my life one perfect rhyme,
Sung to the air of sweet content,
With blended sounds of a life well spent.

—Eloise Alberta Veronica Bibb Thompson (1878–1927)

Born in New Orleans, Eloise Bibb had her first volume of verse published by the time she was seventeen years old. After graduating from Howard University in 1908, she became head resident of the Colored Social Settlement in Washington, D.C., holding the position until 1911. She and her husband, Noah D. Thompson, were devout Catholics, and were active members in the church.

INFANT BAPTISM

What am I going to do with this child, Lord? I wanted a child and you know I love this baby . . . but I'm scared. I feel so inadequate. How can I make sure that my child is brought up right? Lord, I want my child—well, your child, Lord—to be baptized. Lord, let your children be received into your church. Let your child be blessed by the wisdom of the older members of the body of Christ. To know that this precious baby is already loved and accepted and cared for by your grace means so much. The young children and older children will provide so many opportunities for fun and growth. The church, what a family! What a village! Thanks, God, for this symbolic act that reminds me that I am not alone as a parent, nor is my child. Lord, thank you. Thank you, Jesus! I can hardly wait for Sunday to come.

Amen.

—JAMES KING

James King was previously campus minister at Tennessee State University, and he has served in campus ministries for many years. He received his master of divinity degree from Gammon Theological Center. He is father to three children.

BAPTISM

O Gracious Heavenly Creator, as Your darling son Jesus was baptized by John the Baptist and You pronounced through the Holy Spirit, "This is My beloved son in whom I am well pleased," as I go to be baptized in the water, please baptize me with Your Holy Spirit, that I might have power from on high. Thank you, Lord.

Amen.

—REVEREND CHESTINA MITCHELL ARCHIBALD

Matthew 3:11 serves as a reminder of John the Baptist's prophecy: "I indeed baptize you with water unto repentance: but he that cometh after me . . . shall baptize you with the Holy Ghost, and with fire." We give thanks to God for the chance to be renewed by His Spirit, and humbly offer ourselves to Him.

FOR AN ADULT IN ANTICIPATION OF BAPTISM

O Merciful God, I come to this event asking that I might experience Your amazing grace that I know can save even one who is as wayward as I have been. Please, Lord, let the blood of Jesus fall upon me to wash me and make me pure as refined gold. Anoint me, Lord, that I may from this day forward walk in Your righteous way.

Now, Lord, as I go into this water as an outward sign of my inner transformation, be with me now, henceforth and forever more. In the name of Jesus, who has given us new life, I pray.

Amen.

—REVEREND CHESTINA MITCHELL ARCHIBALD

This prayer on the ceremony of baptism was inspired by Romans 1:5a: "We have received grace and apostleship for obedience to the faith." For adults, baptism can act as a complete spiritual rebirth, allowing God's perfect love to wash over them and cleanse them from the inside out.

FOR FIRST COMMUNION

Lord, this Your child comes now for the first time to break the bread of life. May her belief yield much fruit. May this bread and wine symbolizing the body and blood of our Lord and savior, Jesus Christ, cause her to drink of the living water wherein she will never thirst.

Dwell within her now, Holy Spirit. Let this outward act of communion always remind her of the price paid that she might have eternal life.

Amen.

—REVEREND CHESTINA MITCHELL ARCHIBALD

The writing of this prayer was inspired by I Corinthians 10:16: "The cup of blessing which we bless, is it not the communion of the blood of Christ? The bread which we break, is it not the communion of the body of Christ?" The blessed and holy sacrament of communion reminds us of the supreme sacrifice Jesus made for our eternal salvation.

CONFIRMATION IN THE CHURCH

Lord, as I take these vows and am confirmed in the church, let me be confirmed in the church that was established at the Pentecost, where the Holy Spirit descended from heaven above and got into all assembled and began to speak in tongues. Empower me, Lord, that as I begin here in Judea and Jerusalem and Samaria, that I will not stop until I get to the uttermost parts of the world. Your Word is true, and You have said that every knee shall bow and every tongue shall confess that Jesus Christ is Lord. I come at this time to confess Jesus as the Lord of my life. I vow to give to You, Lord, my time, my talent, and my treasure. Bless now, I pray, for I confess my belief in You, God Almighty, my belief in Jesus, Your Son, and my belief in the Holy Spirit.

Amen.

—REVEREND CHESTINA MITCHELL ARCHIBALD

John 17:5 served as inspiration in the writing of this prayer: "And now, O Father, glorify thou me with thine own self with the glory which I had with thee before the world was." When receiving the blessed sacrament of confirmation, we demonstrate our devotion to God, and our dedication to living our lives in accordance to His will.

BENEDICTION

You have been challenged to leave this institution vowing to make a difference in the world. As you go forth from this place, take the loving spirit you have inherited. You will find mountains—climb them; difficulties—overcome them; obstacles—master them. All around you are the great life-giving, life-sustaining forces of the universe. Give yourself to them. Trust them. Lift up your eyes to the hills. Keep them fixed on the highest peaks—and you will always, always find the strength you need to keep moving upward.

God will bless you now and forever more.

And now unto the Creator who art able to keep you from falling and to present you faultless before Thy kingdom, to the all-wise God who has dominion and power, we pray Your blessing as we say Amen and go forth from this place.

—REVEREND CHESTINA MITCHELL ARCHIBALD

In Romans 16:20, the gospel tells us: "And the God of peace shall bruise Satan under your feet shortly. The grace of our Lord, Jesus Christ be with you. Amen." Those who have devoted their lives to God need never fear anything, because He will be holding them gently in His hand, giving them the strength to meet any challenge in their path, as they journey toward His eternal Kingdom.

PRAYER FOR A HUSBAND AND WIFE AFTER REPEATING WEDDING VOWS

Father, in Jesus' name, thank you for granting us access to your presence. I ask of thee for this man and this woman that you bless this union. May your blessing rest and abide on them all the days of their lives. May they consult and acknowledge you for wisdom and understanding to guide their lives. I ask these blessings in Jesus' name.

Amen.

—DR. HENDERSON SPIVEY

Dr. Spivey has been pastor of Glad Tidings Church of God in Christ in Cedartown, Georgia, for sixteen years, and is also currently serving as presiding superintendent of the Marietta District, Central Georgia Jurisdiction, of The Churches of God in Christ—a position he has held for seven years. In addition, he is treasurer of the International Sunday School Department and a member of the National Constitution Committee, where the governing bylaws of the church are examined.

A Prayer on Marriage

O Lord, our creator, redeemer, and sustainer, we praise Your magnificence. We give You all the honor and the glory for the things You have done. It was Your divine wisdom that called for two individuals to come together as one. We know Your blessings are upon the institution of marriage, for it was at the wedding in Cana that Jesus performed His first miracle. We ask today, Lord, that You guide these who have committed themselves to such a relationship. Help them to love one another, to respect one another, and to cherish one another. Lord, help this husband and wife to be quick to seek first Your kingdom and Your righteousness. We thank You once again for bringing such a relationship into being. In the name of Jesus we pray.

Amen.

—Reverend Chestina Mitchell Archibald

The importance of the holy union of marriage is emphasized in Mark 10:9: "What therefore God hath joined together, let no man put asunder." By placing their commitment in God's hands, the married couple can rest assured that He will do everything to bind their love, blessing their relationship and helping to maintain its harmony.

For a Wedding Anniversary

Lord, we have so much in life for which we are thankful. We have truly enjoyed the abundant life that Thou hast promised. Often, we did not have money, but we had things that money could not buy. We had You in our midst, and we had each other.

Now, as we come to celebrate many years together, we dedicate our lives anew to Thee. Continue to bestow upon us Your blessings. In the name of Jesus, we pray.

Amen.

—Reverend Chestina Mitchell Archibald

In this prayer celebrating a wedding anniversary, we are reminded of the glory that is brought only with a loving, trusting, loyal, and dedicated union. As stated in I Corinthians 13:7–8: "Love . . . heareth all things, believeth all things, hopeth all things, endureth all things. Love never faileth."

A GROUNDBREAKING PRAYER

Our Father, it is with hearts of gratitude and thankfulness that we bow before You this day, acknowledging Your greatness and graciousness. By Your providential care You have led us to this point so that we may dedicate this house as a place where Your servant may find rest, reflection, and rejuvenation to do Your will and work.

We thank You for all who have given of themselves, their means, and their concerns to make this plan a reality. By Your grace may this house become a home, and the rooms give rest and refreshment to those who will occupy them.

Through Jesus Christ our Lord, who is the Chief Cornerstone, we pray.

    Amen.

—BENJAMIN S. BAKER

Benjamin S. Baker is a 1970 graduate of the University of Louisville and received his master of divinity, master of religious education, and doctor of ministry degrees from Southern Baptist Theological Seminary. In addition to his work in religious education, he is the author of several books, including *Special Occasions in the Black Church*, which features this prayer. He, his wife, and their four children currently reside in Michigan.

A Prayer for Groundbreaking

O God, for as much as You have given us strength, we realize it is the obligation of each generation to impart its treasures of wisdom and knowledge to the generation following. For the fulfillment of this task, we need not only the best that we as humans can do, but above all the blessing of You, O God. We therefore ask now, Lord, of You who giveth liberally, that You bless this ground that we break in faith. May the structure that is to be built here serve as a monument of Your goodness. Continue to bless our effort that we may bring forth fruit in abundance. In Christ's Name.

Amen.

—Reverend Chestina Mitchell Archibald

Reverend Archibald was inspired by Isaiah 28:16 in writing this prayer: "Therefore thus saith the Lord God, behold, I lay in Zion for a foundation a stone, a tried stone, a precious corner stone, a sure foundation. . . ." As we pray at this groundbreaking for a sturdy foundation that is blessed by God, we recall the way in which He has already given each of us a solid cornerstone of His love and faith, on which we continue to build.

A MEALTIME PRAYER

Dear God, as we bow to offer prayers of gratitude for plenty, remind us that we live in a nation that makes up five percent of the world's population. Yet we consume almost fifty percent of the world's goods and hoard almost forty percent of the world's wealth. Open our hearts that we might see our selfish ways and become truly sorry and repent. Only then will we be able to digest Your food, which is for our souls. As we, however, partake of this bounty of food prepared to nourish the flesh, may the strength we derive from the meals we eat be used for the alleviation of human suffering everywhere. In the Name of Him who never surrendered His soul.

Amen.

—DR. MACK KING CARTER

Dr. Carter received his B.A. degree from the University of Florida and his master of divinity and doctor of divinity degrees from the Southern Baptist Theological Seminary. In addition to preaching, lecturing, and teaching, he has published three books: *A Catechism for Baptist, To Calvary and Beyond,* and *A Quest for Freedom.*

GRACE AT MEALTIME

Father in Heaven: Giver of every
good gift, we thank you for your
gracious provision for our creature needs.
As we partake of the food prepared for
our nourishment, we are mindful of those
who have little or nothing to eat.
May the food strengthen us for your
service this day, and may you be
glorified is our prayer in Jesus' name.
Amen.

—CHARLIE J. JOHNSON

A pastor for thirty-one years, Charlie Johnson, of Sweetwater, Tennessee, says: "I live a prayer life, and try to keep my petitions simple and direct, since God is not impressed with erudition and multiplied words. I also remember to thank Him for what He provides as daily bread, taking nothing for granted."

A SEASON PASS

Lord, today is the opening of the football season—a time that boosts the spirits of many fans throughout our country. Lord, I pray tonight in the spirit of the season that we look to you to be the quarterback of our lives. May we look to your word as our daily living play-book—huddling often with family and friends who are positive and who uplift our spirits.

And when setbacks come our way, we ask your clear direction, Lord, to mold us and keep down the penalties and turnovers of sin in our lives. Through practice may we rid ourselves of the behaviors that keep us from the goals we have and that you have for us.

For I know, Lord, that your love, mercy, and grace is sufficient to help us continue to move the chains forward—continually making first downs on the field of life. May your cheers of support fill our hearts, minds, emotions, and souls—bringing our lives in league with you. With an attitude of gratitude for the crisp cool air of fall and the joyous activities that accompany the season.

Amen.

—COMMANDER JOHN WESLEY MORRISON

Currently assigned in the U.S. Navy as the command chaplain, USS *Theodore Roosevelt* (CVN 71), Commander Morrison is stationed in Norfolk, Virginia. He was ordained an elder in the African Methodist Episcopal Church in 1980, and has received numerous awards, including the Navy Achievement Medal, the National Defense Medal, and the Meritorious Service Medal. On his prayer, he says: "This prayer inspires me to let God be the king and director of my life. Images of God can be found in all of life's situations and circumstances."

OPENING PRAYER FOR A
GENERAL ASSEMBLY

To You, O God, be the glory for the things Thou hast done. O Gracious and Almighty God, Thou who hath created us and called us into existence. Thou who in Thy infinite wisdom has placed in us a soul that cannot rest until it rests in Thee. To you, O Creator, we come just now to acknowledge Your presence and humbly bow before Thee to seek Thy divine guidance for this august body of leaders.

We are reminded in Thy word that if we ask, it shall be given, if we seek, we shall find, and if we knock, doors shall be opened unto us. Lord, we ask that a new spirit of unity, not sameness, permeate this group. Let them know that we all are one in Your spirit, yet this oneness cannot be made manifest until we each attune ourselves to Thee. Lord, we further ask that each will be granted that undeniable courage and creative intellect that will cause them to boldly go forth to do the things that will transform hope into achievement, and will challenge them to move beyond mere perfunctory acts of lawmaking to serious legislation that will effectuate change on the drug scene, child molestation, corruption in high places, aid to the homeless, and have justice to truly roll down like a mighty stream.

Lord, we now knock at Your door of wisdom. Begin now to close the gaps in humanity so that we all may see sparks of divinity in each other. Then and only then will we be able to understand and appreciate and witness the joy, peace, and contentment that Thou hast promised. Let now the words of each person's mouth and meditation of each person's heart be acceptable in Thy sight, O Lord, our strength and our redeemer.

Amen.

—REVEREND CHESTINA MITCHELL ARCHIBALD

This prayer was given by Reverend Archibald before the General Assembly of the state of Tennessee. It was the first time a female had prayed before this body of leaders.

PRAYER FOR A MEETING

Almighty and everlasting God; Thou who art loving, patient, kind, and wonderfully gracious. Thou who hath called us into existence and created us into Thine own image.

Lord, we come today asking that You touch each of these members at the point of their individual needs. Heal all sorrow, pain, and disappointments. Heal all feelings of inadequacy that may cause anyone to unreasonably seek to elevate self, in an effort to compensate notwithstanding the expense. Send Your healing power, Lord. Pull each one to new levels of self-contentment and peace that they may find love, joy, happiness, and much prosperity.

Lord, as we seek Thy wisdom, we find that the faults we most readily find in others are usually reflections of our own weaknesses. Therefore, Lord, strengthen us where we are weak, build us up where we are torn down that we may always seek to do what is pleasing to You. Let now the words of our mouths and the meditations of our hearts be acceptable in Thy sight, O Lord, our strength and our redeemer.

Amen.

—REVEREND CHESTINA MITCHELL ARCHIBALD

The writing of this prayer was influenced by Exodus 25:22: "And there I will meet with thee, and I will commune with thee from above." When we gather with others to call a meeting to order, we may not see what problems each individual may be dealing with inside; we ask God to come to each of these people, blessing them and lifting each one higher.

NEGOTIATIONS

O Lord who is both just and fair, we call on Your spirit of equity to guide us this day. As we sit in negotiations, we ask that You serve as a moderator. Convict us if we step outside of an attitude of love, justice, and equity. Help us to interact as Christians who hold Your will as the ultimate priority. Work through us, Lord, that we may all leave the table satisfied with the results of the meeting. Above all, we pray that in these negotiations none of our wills be done apart from Yours. In the name of Jesus, we pray.

     Amen.

—REVEREND CHESTINA MITCHELL ARCHIBALD

We are told in Proverbs 10:4: "He becometh poor that dealeth with a slack hand: but the hand of the diligent maketh rich." In today's world, many people often lose sight of what is truly important in life. With God's help, we will act in ways that demonstrate our loyalty to Him and show that we are indeed His children.

For a Luncheon

God of goodness, graciousness, and generosity, we thank you for the grandeur of this banquet, the bounty of your blessings, and for the beauty of those unselfish persons who will be honored here this day. In the age of scarcity, replenish our resources with economic vitality and the fertility of selfless sharing. Teach us that if we give to be rewarded we incorrectly see you as our Divine Santa Claus. If we give so that we can claim an exemption on our tax return, we incorrectly see you as our Divine CPA. If we give so that we impress others, we expect you to be our Divine Public Relations Agent. But, if we give because we are philanthropists, then we correctly know you as a God of love.

Amen.

—Dr. J. Alfred Smith, Sr.

Dr. Smith, senior pastor of Allen Temple Baptist Church in Oakland, California, has traveled extensively to speak at churches and seminaries nationwide, and has also been a guest lecturer at numerous universities. He is the author of sixteen inspirational books, which are used around the world by seminaries, Bible students, teachers, and scholars.

A LUNCHEON PRAYER

Almighty God of heaven and earth, east and west, male and female, Jew and Gentile, we come right now to acknowledge You as the Alpha and Omega. Realizing that You are omnipresent, Your spirit abides in each of us and with all of us right now.

Creator, in Your word You have said that if we ask it shall be given. We come this afternoon asking that You pour out Your Holy Spirit on this luncheon as we seek to honor one who loves and adores You—one who values time, who finds pleasure in working and dignity in simplicity, and who understands worth in character, power in kindness, influence of example, obligations of duty, wisdom of economy, and virtue of patience.

We seek Your divine guidance in all that is said and done here today. And we knock at Your door of wisdom asking that You continue to imbue our hearts with love that she may continue to increase in true beauty and remain graceful, virtuous as one who has been called to rise above mediocrity to be an example for others to follow. In Christ's Name.

  Amen.

—REVEREND CHESTINA MITCHELL ARCHIBALD

This prayer was given at an appreciation luncheon for Dr. Eunice W. Ponder. The prayer reminds us that God works through each of us, giving some extraordinary individuals the wisdom and strength to soar above mediocre standards.

Prayers for Holidays and Other Special Days

Delight thyself also in the Lord; and he shall give thee the desires of thine heart.

A PRAYER ON MARTIN LUTHER KING JR.'S BIRTHDAY
January 15th

Oh, God, when days were dark deed,
When we were fast in Slavery's chain,
Thou then our parents' prayers did heed
And helped us freedom to obtain.

And when adrift upon the world
A child race 'mid the great and strong,
Thy banner o'er was unfurled
And gently we were led along.

Help us ever to remember Thee
And ever to endless homage pay
For all the great prosperity
Enjoyed by our race today.

—KATHERINE DAVIS CHAPMAN TILLMAN (1870– ?)

Katherine Davis Chapman Tillman was a poet who grew up in the Dakotas. Her articles appeared in publications such as *Christian Recorder* and the *Indianapolis Freeman*.

IN MEMORIAM FREDERICK DOUGLASS

O Death! Why dost thou steal the great,
With grudging like to strongest hate,
And rob the world of giant minds,
For whom all nature mourns and pines.

So few have upon the earth,
Whom God ennobled at their birth,
With genius stamped upon their souls,
That guides, directs, persuades, controls.

So few who scorn the joys of life,
And labor in contending strife,
With zeal increased and strength of ten,
To ameliorate the ills of men.

So few who keep a record clean,
Amid temptations strong and keen;
Who live laborious days and nights,
And shun the storms of passion's blight.

O, why cannot these linger here.
As light upon this planet drear;
Forever in the public sight,
To lead us always to the right.

—ELOISE ALBERTA VERONICA BIBB THOMPSON (1878–1927)

Eloise Bibb, best known for writing poetry on biblical and historical subjects and romantic narratives, was an active member of the Catholic Church. In addition to her poetry, she wrote features for newspapers such as the *Los Angeles Sunday Tribune*, and contributed articles to popular magazines.

COMMEMORATIVE PRAYER FOR
W. E. B. DU BOIS' BIRTHDAY
February 23rd

––––––

O Gracious and Almighty God, Thou who hath no respect of person and thus imbues each of us with unique gifts. We gather today to commemorate the birth of one who used his gifts in a self-sacrificing manner in order that future generations would have an appreciation for learning. He not only persistently demanded excellence in education for himself and others, but served as the perfect example of the pursuit of excellence.

Now, Lord, as we commemorate the birth of William Edward Burghardt Du Bois, may we but obtain a little of his unwavering faith in the blood of our ancestors, in order that we, too, may be strengthened to serve the causes of truth and freedom. May we each learn that true freedom comes only when we are able to go or come home to self as Du Bois learned only in his latter days.

Amen.

—REVEREND CHESTINA MITCHELL ARCHIBALD

This prayer was given by Reverend Archibald at Fisk University, which is the alma mater of W. E. B. Du Bois. The prayer serves as a memorial to one of the most extraordinary African Americans in history, and reminds us of the early struggles fought for the freedom we enjoy today.

A Lenten Prayer

Dear God, as we begin this season (journey) of Lent, help us not to rush too quickly to the empty tomb. Let us remember that there was no resurrection without first going through the wilderness, going through the cross. There is no triumph without seeking God's face, without submitting our way to God's will. Help me during this time of rededication, as I open my existence to you through discipline, prayer and fasting to listen to your guidance that I might follow your will now and forever more.

Amen.

—Reverend Lillian C. Smith

Reverend Smith is currently chaplain-director of the Wesley Foundation, the United Methodist Campus Ministry of Howard University, in Washington, D.C. She also serves as an associate minister at Asbury United Methodist Church, and is responsible for Youth and Young Adult Ministries.

A PRAYER FOR EASTER SUNDAY

Thanks be to you, O God. Thanks, because the terror of evil has ended. And the power and the glory are yours, forever and ever. Thanks be to you, O God. For after the desertion of the disciples and the betrayal of Judas, for after the bloody violence of the crucifixion and the painful death and burial of Jesus Christ for our sins, you are still God. You are the God who raised Jesus from the dead on this day. On this day of victory over death, hell, and the grave, we come rejoicing. On Friday Satan shot his best shot, killing our Lord and Savior, but on this day heaven and earth rejoice because you nullified the work of the devil. On this day light defeated darkness, truth overcame falsehood, salvation triumphed over sin.

We pray that on this day there will be a brand new beginning for all of us. Grant that our ugly pasts will be buried and that we might arise in the newness of life as new people who are making a fresh and genuine new commitment to walk with the risen Christ. May the risen Christ save lost souls, convert us sinners, and teach us that we are no longer captives to the sins which bind and blind us. Have mercy on the sick and suffering. Heal those who are physically, mentally, and spiritually sick. Comfort the bereaved and grief-stricken. Empty out tombs of despair, discouragement, and defeat. Resurrect us with resurrection power. Raise us to new levels of powerful and victorious living. Bless the preaching of your Holy Word. Burn our altars of prayer with the fire of the Holy Ghost. Give us the boldness to tell the world that Jesus, our savior, is not a dead but the living Lord of history. In Jesus' name, we pray.

   Amen.

—Dr. J. Alfred Smith, Sr.

In light of his many great accomplishments, Dr. Smith has been the recipient of more than 125 awards and honors. Among these acknowledgments, he was selected one of America's fifteen greatest African American preachers by *Ebony* magazine in 1993, and was named 1994 Outstanding Citizen of the Year by the *Oakland Tribune.*

AN EASTER PRAYER

The mystery of your presence is manifest today. We rejoice with the angels in heaven at your victory, for in your victory, we have victory. For in your triumph, the wisdom of God's plan is made known. God has restored humankind unto thine self. Communication channels between God and God's people are renewed. God has fulfilled God's prophecy and proved that indeed God is sovereign.

—DENEISE C. JACK

Deneise Jack is a coproducer and editor of two television shows. Originally from New Orleans, Louisiana, she is currently a resident of Nashville, Tennessee.

A PENTECOST PRAYER

Dear Comforter, Teacher, Guide, Jesus said you were coming. You entered into our lives in such a grandiose style. You left many speechless and others speaking the mighty word of God. Since your arrival no one has been the same. Many were saved at your appearance and today your presence engulfs the world. You are so wonderful, Lord, and you came bearing so many gifts—tools we need today to bless the body of Christ. Today I choose to decrease my self-interest so that you may increase within me.

Amen.

—DENEISE C. JACK

Deneise C. Jack is Christian education director at Victory Baptist Church in Nashville, Tennessee. Her prayer reminds us to continually thank God for blessing us with the Holy Spirit, a gift which can compare to no other.

MOTHER'S DAY PRAYER

O God, the mother of all living beings, the creator of the universe and the giver of all good things. We thank you for our home on earth and for the joy of living. By your divine wisdom you have made mothers the bearers of new life on earth.

As we worship, O Lord, call to our minds the magnificent and gracious gifts that you have bestowed upon mothers. We thank you for their love, their forbearance, their patience and their unselfishness. And we pray that all mothers may be the bearers of love that you have so graciously shared in the gift of your Son, Jesus Christ, for our salvation.

Amen.

—DR. THOMAS KILGORE, JR.

Dr. Kilgore is pastor emeritus of the Second Baptist Church, the oldest black Baptist church in Los Angeles, California. He has received honorary degrees from Shaw University, Morehouse College, and the University of Southern California. In his prayer, we are reminded of the love we have received from our mothers and the eternal gratitude we have toward them for showing us kindness and affection as they support us in all ways.

A MEMORIAL DAY PRAYER

O God, we come on this Memorial Day to commemorate the many men and women who have died fighting in wars so that the citizens of this country can be free. Bless this day the families of those who are no longer with them in body. I pray this prayer in the remembrance of Jesus, who gave His life so that all might be free and have the right to eternal life. May those whose lives were given for justice, freedom, and righteousness, be not given in vain, but that the cause for which they died will become a reality.

Amen.

—REVEREND CHESTINA MITCHELL ARCHIBALD

The theme of this prayer is based in part on Isaiah 9:7a: "Of the increase of his government and peace there shall be no end. . . ." When we remember those who have died in wars, we also pray for God to help the people of this world to spread peace, so that we may work out our differences in the future without weapons, without bloodshed.

A SPECIAL PRAYER FOR MEMORIAL DAY

Lord, many in our country today will celebrate Memorial Day in various fashions. Many will remember those who have died in battles at home and abroad. Yet, today we come to commemorate those who fought for freedom abroad and had to come home and fight for equal rights here. Many of these have died on the streets of many of our cities out of hurt and anger. Many have died from overdoses of drugs used to wipe their pain and hurt away. Bless their memories. Preserve the best thoughts about them in the memories of their loved ones. In Jesus' name, we pray.

Amen.

—REVEREND CHESTINA MITCHELL ARCHIBALD

Reverend Archibald was inspired by Ephesians 6:12 in the writing of this prayer: "For me wrestle not against flesh and blood, but against principalities, against powers, against the rulers of darkness of this world, against spiritual wickedness in high places." Fighting against institutions and ideas as Martin Luther King, Jr., did can effectively and peacefully bring about a positive change, but God is saddened when He sees His own children warring against each other.

Prayer on Juneteenth

Dear Lawd,

We heard down here today in Texas that Lincoln freed the slaves
down there in Washington. We heard today, Lawd, that it
happened over two years ago.

But freedom ain't just saying it, Lawd.
Freedom ain't just writin' it, Lawd.
Freedom is doin' it, too . . .

And they only did it here in Texas, Lawd
On June the nineteenth.

Some say, Lawd, that Black folk ain't on time, they in time.
But we say, Lawd, ain't nevah too late for freedom.

And while Mistah Lincoln spozed to free us.
It didn't just happen here, Lawd . . .

We thank you, Lawd, for Mistah Lincoln,
But we also thank you, Lawd, that we been free in our minds a
mighty long time . . .

Yes Lawd, freedom ain't just saying it, Lawd,
Freedom ain't just writin' it, Lawd,
Freedom is doin' it, too . . .

An' hit finally been done to us here in Texas, Lawd,
On Juneteenth.

  Amen.

—Dr. Raymond A. Winbush

In this prayer, a modern man expresses the point of view of a Texas slave who first heard about Lincoln's Emancipation Proclamation two years after its declaration. Currently director of race relations at Fisk University in Nashville, Tennessee, Dr. Winbush is deeply rooted in African American traditions. He has traveled extensively and is extremely knowledgeable in the area of African American studies.

PRAYER ON JUNETEENTH

O God, our creator, Thou who only art Holy and Righteous, Thou who art almighty and all powerful, Thou who move men to act, when in themselves they dare not; it is You, our savior, that we Your Ebony Children come today to acknowledge, praise, and forever give thanks, because we have witnessed Your direct intervention on our behalf. Today, we remember Your faithfulness to our cause of freedom. May the delay in our ancestors' discovery in Texas of the signing of the Emancipation Proclamation—January 1, 1863—always remind us that knowledge is freedom and ignorance can be hell. Lord, grant us now Your wisdom and Your strength to forever pursue truth and freedom.

In the mighty name of Jesus, we pray and offer thanks anew.

　　Amen.

—REVEREND CHESTINA MITCHELL ARCHIBALD

The theme of this prayer is found in Exodus 14:13a, 14: "Fear ye not, stand still, and see the salvation of the Lord. . . . The Lord shall fight for you, and ye shall hold your peace." With God's help, may we have the courage and wisdom to endeavor to bring about freedom for all people in all nations, so that they, too, may know what it means to be liberated.

A FATHER'S DAY PRAYER

Eternal and infinite God, we have at times been faithless and indifferent, but we come to thee now with a child's confidence and expectancy. We come to our Father's heart of forgiveness, to our Father's mind for instruction, and to our Father's strength for protection. We thank you for our earthly fathers who have provided homes in which it was good to be reared. We thank you for fathers who are never too weary to show kindness, never too selfish to give love, and never too busy to share time. May all fathers be wise, prudent, and honorable, and may they always strive to do right and keep their faith in Thee.

   Amen.

—Dr. Thomas Kilgore, Jr.

Dr. Kilgore is a graduate of Morehouse College and Union Theological Seminary. In 1971, he was chosen the first black president of the American Baptist Convention. His prayer reminds us that on Father's Day we give thanks for the men who provided us with loving homes as we grew up. We remember the values they instilled in us, and we remain forever appreciative for being fortunate enough to have been so blessed.

For the Fourth of July

Lord, thank You for allowing us to live in a country where we can serve, honor, and praise Thee without undue influence, control, or determination of government. Thank You, Lord, for a Declaration of Independence. May we forever remain independent of anything but Thee. In Thy true spirit of freedom that only You can grant. Amen.

—Reverend Chestina Mitchell Archibald

The importance of freedom, particularly religious freedom, is echoed in Isaiah 61:1: "The spirit of the Lord God is upon me; because the Lord hath anointed me to preach good tidings unto the meek; he hath sent me to bind up the brokenhearted, to proclaim liberty to the captives, and the opening of the prison to them that are bound." This prayer gives thanks to God for the liberty we enjoy daily in this country, and reminds us that we must not take it for granted.

A LABOR DAY PRAYER

Heavenly Father, in the name of Jesus Christ of Nazareth and by the power of His blood given to us as Christians, I come before you to offer a few words of thanks: I thank You, "For we are [Your] workmanship, created in Christ Jesus for good works, which [You] prepared beforehand, that we should walk in them" (Ephesians 2:10). And I also thank You that, "It is [Your] gift to man that every one should eat and drink and take pleasure in all his toil" (Ecclesiastes 3:13). Father, I ask that You compass and aid all those who toil and labor with or without hope, for those who are underpaid and find it difficult to pay their bills, for those who labor for little profit or gain, for all those who have families to support and those who look in vain for work. Also for those who take advantage of others in their misfortunes. I pray for Your forgiveness, grace, mercy, and redeeming power. I likewise pray that the spirit of the Lord will rest upon men and women of integrity and honesty, who do not lack godly wisdom concerning others and themselves.

Please guide and protect all who work for fair and equal wages in our society, and help us all who realize that, "Whatever [our] task, work heartily, as serving the Lord and not men, knowing that from the Lord [we] will receive the inheritance as [our] reward; [we] are serving the Lord Christ" (Colossians 3:23–24).

Now, help us to value and find purpose in the work You have given us and use us as instruments of Your divine will, so that we may serve and work with You; in Jesus' holy name we pray.

   Amen.

—REVEREND ROOSEVELT HUGHES, JR.

A native of Mississippi, Reverend Hughes is currently serving at John Street Baptist Church, in Wooster, Massachusetts—the oldest African American Baptist Church in the country. His ministry focuses on assisting the homeless.

A THANKSGIVING PRAYER

Give us thankful hearts, O God, in this the season of Thy Thanksgiving. May we be thankful for health and strength, for sun and rain and peace. Let us seize the day and opportunity to strive for that greatness of spirit that measures life not by its disappointments but by its possibilities, and let us ever remember that true gratitude and appreciation shows itself neither in independence nor satisfaction but passes the gift joyfully on in larger and better form. Such gratitude grant us, O Lord.

Amen.

—W. E. B. DU BOIS (1868–1963)

In addition to his many other accomplishments, W. E. B. Du Bois received two B.A. degrees from Fisk University, in Nashville, Tennessee, and acquired a doctorate degree from Harvard University. After an extensive career working for civil rights reform in America, he migrated to Africa in 1961, becoming editor-in-chief of the *Encyclopedia Africana*.

PRAYERS FOR A KWANZAA CELEBRATION
(December 26–January 1)

Kwanzaa is a secular African American holiday celebrated from December 26 through January 1. Created by Dr. Maulana Karenga in 1966, Kwanzaa transcends ideological, regional, and class boundaries. Kwanzaa, or "first fruits," commemorates African celebrations of the first harvest wherein the Creator is thanked for the blessing of food and sustenance. Intended to reaffirm and restore our African heritage, Kwanzaa also seeks to reinforce the bond among African Americans through commitment to values and community. Each day represents the celebration of a different principle of the Nguzu Saba ("seven values" in Kiswahhili). Formal celebration of Kwanzaa includes candle lighting, feasts, and the exchange of gifts and libations from a unity cup. The essence of Kwanzaa involves an individual and communal commitment to the edification of the African American community. As a spiritual people, we celebrate Kwanzaa with the fervor and sanctity of prayer.

A GENERAL PRAYER FOR KWANZAA

May we set aside this time of year to commit and recommit ourselves and our resources to the up-building of the African American community. May our prayers speak equally to our God, our families, and our own hearts as commitments to serve and to act. Let us pray.

Day One: Umoja (Unity)

Unity—we must strive for and maintain unity in the family, community, nation, and race. *Behold how good it is for brothers and sisters to dwell together in unity. Psalms 133:1*

Lord, we come before You committing our hearts in unity to each other through You. May You grant us loving hearts, forgiving spirits, and open minds to accept and treasure those You have placed around us. May we find beauty in all Your creation as we strive toward togetherness in every aspect of the community—from the deepest corners of the African Diaspora to our own neighbors and siblings. May Your peace bring us together.

Day Two: Kujichagulia (Self-Determination)

Self-determination—to define ourselves, name ourselves, create for ourselves, and speak for ourselves instead of being defined, named, created, and spoken for by others. *A good name is rather to be chosen than great riches, and loving favor rather than silver and gold. Proverbs 22:1*

Lord, we stand strong in the knowledge of ourselves in You, in You, we know that we are a chosen generation, a royal priesthood, and people who are more than conquerors over those who deny us voice and agency. May we find within ourselves the devotion to remain dedicated to our development and growth. May Your love give us power to define.

DAY THREE: UJIMA
(COLLECTIVE WORK AND RESPONSIBILITY)

The purpose of this day is to build and maintain our community together and make our sister's and brother's problems our problems and solve them together. *Look not every person on his or her own things, but every one on the things of others. Philippians 2:4*

Lord, we are determined to be our brother's and sister's keeper for You. We pledge to feed the hungry, give drink to the thirsty, clothe the naked, and take in strangers we find around us. May we be conscious of the joys and the struggles of those in our community, and celebrate and weep as though they are our own. May Your model of hospitality become our communal responsibility.

DAY FOUR: UJAMAA
(COOPERATIVE ECONOMICS)

A day centered on the planning, building, and maintaining of our own stores, shops, and other businesses, and to profit from them together. *Two are better than one; because they have a good reward for their labor. Ecclesiastes 4:9*

Lord, we acknowledge that we all need support in order to grow. We need Your strength, Your encouragement, and Your people. May we, therefore, patronize each other in order to grow and prosper— even if it means forsaking individual convenience and popularity. May Your wisdom teach us to nurture each other.

DAY FIVE: NIA (PURPOSE)

Purpose—to make our collective vocation building and developing our community to restore our people to their traditional greatness. *I told them that the hand of God had been gracious upon me, and also the words that the king has spoken to me. Then they said, "Let's start building!" So they committed themselves to the common good. Nehemiah 2:18*

Lord, we find the strength to build and rebuild in Your promises of restoration. We vow to center our lives in a purpose that treasures the common good, and works towards its fulfillment. May we be ever mindful of the glories and tragedies of our past; and may they inspire us to construct our collective even further. May Your faithfulness encourage us.

DAY SIX: KUUMBA (CREATIVITY)

This day focuses on always doing as much as we can in order to leave our community more beautiful and beneficial than when we inherited it. *God has given each of you special gifts and abilities; be sure to use them to help each other, passing on to others God's many kind blessings. I Peter 4:10*

Lord, we treasure the unique gifts that You have given to each of us. Today we covenant to utilize our talents to help each other and beautify our surroundings. May we share our own discoveries and abilities with our brothers and sisters that we may give birth, rather than destroy, and plant rather than tear down. May Your Spirit inspire us.

DAY SEVEN: IMANI (FAITH)

The final day of Kwanzaa concentrates on faith and the desire to believe with all our hearts, in our people, our teachers, our leaders, and the righteousness and victory of our struggle. *For faith is substance of things hoped for, and evidence of things not seen. Hebrews 11:1*

Lord, we know all things are possible in the tenacity of faith. When we can not hear Your voice or see Your face, live out our dreams or envision the future, we press forward in our belief in You, ourselves, and each other. No matter the obstacle or discouragement, may we always have the faith to believe in the soldiers who fight, and the righteousness of the struggle. May Your assurance give us energy.

—REVEREND MONICA A. COLEMAN

Graduating magna cum laude from Harvard-Radcliffe College, Reverend Coleman is cofounder and former editor-in-chief of *Revival Journal*. She is presently matriculating at Vanderbilt Divinity School in Nashville, Tennessee, serving as the minister of history of the National Alliance of Pan-African Seminarians.

YULETIDE PRAYER

O Gracious God, unto us a Son You have given, unto us a child has been born. We call him Wonderful Counselor, Prince of Peace.

We gather throughout this season in fellowship in remembrance of this Your gift to us, knowing that it is only through our belief in Him that we can really experience joy in this world.

Bless now each of us. Heal our unbelief—strengthen our faith that we may experience the true meaning of Christmas.

Lord, bless this bounty of food that has been prepared. Make us ever-mindful of those less fortunate, and undergird us with Thy power that we may forget self enough to go out spreading good tidings to others. In the Name of Jesus, we pray.

　　　Amen.

—REVEREND CHESTINA MITCHELL ARCHIBALD

Each year at Fisk University, the entire Fisk family (the faculty and staff, along with their families) gathers to celebrate Christmas. This prayer was written in December 1987, when Reverend Archibald's son, Albert John Archibald, recited the prayer for the occasion for the first time.

A CHRISTMAS PRAYER

Lord, this day is your day. This day, I make time to bless you. For today I'm reminded that it was you who left the safety of your father's heaven and lowered yourself as a servant for me. It was you, precious Savior, who provided humans that opportunity to live again. Oh, generous Son of God, how marvelous you are. For you knew that many would reject you. Nevertheless, you were still willing to come and die for us. Today I bless you, Dear Lord. I'll tell the world the story of your goodness, forgiveness, and mercy; and the hope of glory.

—DENEISE C. JACK

Deneise C. Jack recently returned to continue her education by matriculating at Tennessee State University, where she is majoring in mass communications. Her prayer describes how at Christmas, we have an opportunity to reflect on the glorious miracle that was sent to us from God in the form of His son, Jesus.

ON CHRISTMAS

O Mary's baby, born in a manger, came into the world by no fault or choice of your own. Yet, the whole host of heaven rejoiced at your birth, for you were born without sin that you may take on the sins of the world. Lord, we come today to celebrate your birthday. May we go forth showing your love today. May the gifts that we exchange not be for show, form or fashion, but merely to show another that we care as you care for us. In your precious name, Jesus, we pray.

    Amen.

—REVEREND LILLIAN C. SMITH

A resident of Upper Marlboro, Maryland, Reverend Smith graduated cum laude from the Wesley Theological Seminary in Washington, D.C. Responding to her calling from God, she has "a deep commitment to working for justice, love, and kindness."

FOR THE NEW YEAR

Our father and Our God, we come to you thanking you for the old year. For some it was a year of successes and the realization of dreams. For some it was a year of failure and broken dreams. For some it was a year of sorrow and some of it we would rather forget but we made it. There are some of us who made it to the threshold of this day but didn't make it. Some fell by the wayside. We realize that if it hadn't been for you shielding us, protecting us and your healing mercies we too would have been among the fallen. But because of your grace we made it to another year. Last year we were not all that we should have been. We were not all we could have been. We made some mistakes. Forgive us, Lord. As we enter into the new year we like Paul are "forgetting those things which are behind, and reaching forth unto those things which are before, I press toward the mark for the prize of the high calling of God in Christ Jesus." Guide our steps Oh Lord in this new year so that we would go in the direction that is pleasing in your sight. That we would go into the highway and byways spreading your word and your love. Help us to take our eyes off man, things, and position, and seek first the things of the kingdom. We ask your blessing upon our lives and the lives of our loved ones, our leaders and our nation. We have before us a new year, one that has not been marred by our human frailties. Help us to live lives that would bring glory to your name and that our lives will be a testimony to your goodness and grace. We pray that lives would be saved not because of who we are but whose we are. In Jesus's name we pray.

Amen.

—REVEREND CATHERINE H. REED

Reverend Reed is associate minister at the John Street Baptist Church, in Wooster, Massachusetts. The church is the oldest African American Baptist Church in the country.

A Prayer for the New Year

Help us to remember, O Lord, in this beginning of the year that the man who makes and breaks his New Year's resolves is at least better than the man who makes none. Deliver us from such sloth and self-satisfaction as see no evil and recognize no possible improvement or are too lazy to attempt the good. Give us courage to fail in a good cause, and determination never to cease striving toward that which God, His world and our own hearts tell us is worthwhile. Wherefore, O Lord, shall the world count its steps from that dark cross on Calvary, if those steps be not really toil and slipping and back-sliding and yet withal that forward-coming toward Thee.

Amen.

—W. E. B. Du Bois (1868–1963)

Many books are part of the remarkable legacy of W. E. B. Du Bois, including *The Suppression of the Slave Trade* (1896), *The Souls of Black Folk* (1903), and *Black Flame* (1957–1961). Between 1897 and 1914, he conducted many sociological studies of black society in America, and published sixteen research papers. He concluded that in a climate of racial hostility, social change could only be accomplished by agitation and protest.

INDEX

Note: Titles of prayers are in upper and lower case, names of authors are all in capitals